DEMYSTIFYING THE COUNSELING PROCESS

What was the most
exciting experiance
you had over the
last week?

DEMYSTIFYING THE COUNSELING PROCESS

A Self-Help Handbook for Counselors

ARLENE KING

Montclair State University

ALLYN AND BACON

Boston ■ London ■ Toronto ■ Sydney ■ Tokyo ■ Singapore

Vice President: *Paul A. Smith*
Senior Editor: *Virginia Lanigan*
Editorial Assistant: *Jennifer Conners*
Marketing Managers: *Brad Parkins, Kathleen Morgan*
Editorial Production Service: *Chestnut Hill Enterprises, Inc.*
Manufacturing Buyer: *Suzanne Lareau*
Cover Administrator: *Kristina Mose-Libon*

Copyright © 2001 by Allyn & Bacon
A Pearson Education Company
160 Gould Street
Needham Heights, MA 02494

Internet: www.abacon.com

Between the time Website information is gathered and published, some sites may
have closed. Also, the transcription of URLs can result in typographical errors. The
publisher would appreciate notification where these occur so that they may be
corrected in subsequent editions.

Library of Congress Cataloging-in-Publication Data

King, Arlene.
    Demystifying the counseling process : a self-help handbook for counselors /
Arlene King.
       p.   cm
    Includes bibliographical references.
    ISBN 0-321-04050-3
    1. Counseling.   I. Title.

BF637.C6 K52 2000
158'.3—dc21

                                                                    00-062068

Printed in the United States of America
10 9 8 7 6 5 4 3 2 1   05 04 03 02 01 00

To the art of counseling, the artists-in-training, and their future benefactors

CONTENTS

PREFACE

Demistifying the Counseling Process is intended primarily for those counselors-in-training who have already studied basic counseling theories and techniques. The focus of the material is to assist in the transition from textbook study to the application of knowledge and skills to real clients in the world beyond the classroom. It is therefore most appropriate that this text be used with students participating in field experiences and those individuals who are striving to "fine-tune" in practice what they have learned in theory.

Much of what is presented is a way of looking at issues in counseling that are regarded as professionally important. Some of what is presented are subtleties of effective counseling that are rarely addressed. This text would also be useful in the area of self-help for practicing counselors. The material highlights areas of counseling techniques that provide structure for further professional development of counselors employed in schools, agencies, business and industry, and private practice.

It is written conversationally and with relative informality and intended to provide a catalyst for the critical assessment and improvement of counseling skills.

ACKNOWLEDGMENTS

I want to thank the teachers, mentors, colleagues, and supervisors from whom I have learned a great deal over the years. Included in this group are not only those individuals who modeled the behaviors that I have chosen to emulate but also those who, however unwittingly, provided models of behaviors that I have chosen not to follow. Experiencing what does not work effectively or what does not fit my value system has sometimes been a strong influence on me.

My sincere gratitude to my counseling students who have shared with me the bumps and bruises of their training, who have pointed out to me what they have found most useful, and who have encouraged me to get my thoughts on paper beyond the notes that they have taken in class.

My greatest vote of thanks goes to over twenty years of clients who have taught me more than they will ever know and without whom there would not have been a reality check for my counseling process.

I also want to thank my editor and the following reviewers of my text, all of whom provided feedback and raised questions that helped to bring clarity and focus to my message: Abigail Bergsma, California State University–Fresno; Paul A. Gore, Southern Illinois University; Becky J. Liddle, Auburn University; Chris McCarthy, University of Texas at Austin; Victoria Manion-Fleming, Miami University; Charles V. Pryor, Northeast Louisiana University; Tim Roberts, Indiana State University; and H. Dan Smith, California State University–Fresno. I particularly appreciate their willingness to accept my desire to personalize my text so that I might present what I have learned from my journey in the counseling profession.

DEMYSTIFYING THE
COUNSELING PROCESS

CHAPTER 1

WHAT'S IT ALL ABOUT?

My primary objective in writing this book is to demystify the counseling process and the role of the counselor for those professionals whose clientele is more like themselves than it is different. Clients who resemble counselors are people who have difficult decisions to make in their lives. They are people who have occasion to face frustration, disappointment, chance, loss, sadness, and unforeseen opportunities. They require the skills needed to cope effectively with these circumstances. They are very much like me and I suspect that they are also like you.

They may come from seriously dysfunctional families or they may not. They may have experienced major traumas in their lives or they may not. They come to us because they need help *now* so they can move forward in their lives more effectively and with more pleasure than pain. This, in effect, constitutes an immediate bond between "us" and "them."

As I see it, these clients come to us seeking better management tools, more successful communication skills, guidelines for making more effective decisions, and a greater sense of control over their lives. They often come to us believing that they have a multitude of problems when perhaps what they are lacking are the tools that would minimize a myriad of difficult circumstances. They come to counseling seeking the skills that we may have internalized for ourselves or because we have at least become knowledgeable enough to teach them to others. For the most part, they are ordinary people, young and old and of a variety of cultures and subcultures, struggling to make happier and more fulfilling lives for themselves. They are very much like you and me. They come to us so that we can work together and that they may leave with an improved quality of life.

Therefore, I want to be clear from the onset that, while I believe that the basic tenets of what I present here will pertain to counseling relationships in general, I fully recognize that more structured, more analytical, and more clinical processes will be required with severely disturbed clients. It is the responsibility of the professional counselor to recognize the differences between the lack of coping skills and clinical depression; between ineffective decision-making and personality disorders; between generalized anxiety and paranoia; between habits and obsessive-compulsive behaviors.

The preparatory study of personality development and psychological disorders for counselors-in-training was designed to yield the knowledge that would enable us to recognize when we, as counselors, are beyond our training and when we, therefore, must make referrals to those professionals with the appropriate clinical expertise. This is not a counselor's weakness. Knowing when to do this, is, in fact, a counselor's strength and it is morally, ethically, legally, and professionally appropriate.

My intent is also not to attempt to construct a new theory of counseling or to give new labels to those proven and helpful theories that you have studied (probably more than once). My aim is to leave the theoretical construct(s) as your choice and to attempt to influence the manner, style, and the process of your relationship with your client and to help you utilize significantly helpful counseling tools. I will say, though, that if you identify yourself as an eclectic counselor who draws from a variety of theories that you deem as appropriate, I hope beyond hope that you do this based on your thorough knowledge of the constructs, not because you're "flying by the seat of your pants."

If your goal is to learn how to more effectively facilitate the process of helping others learn how to help themselves, or if, in fact, you would like to enhance your own life skills, this may be the book to read. If your dream, personally or professionally, however privately held, is to be the sage of all wisdom, the savior of people with problems who don't know all that you do, this book is not for you.

I believe that there is an implicit arrogance in any contention that we have the right to tell anyone how to live their life. I personally resent receiving advice from people who will not be sharing in the consequences of their well-intentioned solution to a problem that I may be facing. My gratitude goes to those who will work with me so that I can accept my past, clarify my goals and think through my options, and encourage me to acknowledge my strengths so that I will be better able to minimize my weaknesses in the future. This facilitative process ultimately helps me arrive at solutions to my problems and that success then belongs to me. I believe that these are the people who are offering effective counseling as they assist me through a process of *my* exploration toward *my* resolution of *my* problem. I then own the consequences of my choices, whether positive or negative. That ownership yields a sense of empowerment that can only enhance my personal development.

Whatever your present position may be, I hope that you will indulge my desire to share with you some of what I have learned and accepted as means for rounding off some of the sharp edges that I brought to counseling when I first began my career. Over the course of time, I have designed and redesigned my techniques repeatedly based on what seemed to be most effective with my clients. Some of what I've integrated into my methodology may raise some questions or provide some answers worthy of your consideration. We may agree. We may disagree. Isn't that what professionals do much of the time? Whatever the outcome, we surely must continually critique what we do and be open to learning from different perspectives. We can all grow with ideas. Welcome to my continuing journey!

After decades of reading texts, taking courses, attending workshops, seeing clients in private practice, teaching counselors-in-training, supervising counselors in the field, and reflecting, reflecting, and reflecting on the questions of what the client wants and what I have to offer, here are some of my observations and objectives for your consideration.

- Clients often feel overwhelmed by a multitude of problems.

  I help them to understand that often there is one (or perhaps a few) problem(s) that turns up in multiple ways and various places.

- Clients often want magical and immediate "cures."

  I help them commit to work because I know of no magic yet uncovered.

- Clients most often want to change the behavior of others.

  I help them to respond in new ways to the behavior of others, which is all that they can really control.

- Clients often want guarantees.

  I help them live with ambiguity because there are so few absolutes in life.

- Clients want to rewrite history.

  I help them begin a new chapter where tomorrow's history begins today.

- Clients want to predict the future.

  I help them develop the transferable skills for coping with what we cannot foresee.

- Clients determine their choices based on what they have accepted as their values.

  I help them examine their values and the pleasures/pains they generate so that they can determine the path that will be most rewarding to them.

- Clients implement only the choices they have made for themselves.

  I help them test and evaluate their commitments because little change comes from words alone.

- Clients have the answers, not me.

  I help them learn how to find their answers because life can be a long journey of problem solving that they will travel without me.

All in all, as an effective counselor, I strive to be the best facilitative educator that I can be, an educator

- Without a lectern;
- Without judgments of good and bad;
- Who is a temporary partner in the exploration of the client's world;
- Who models skills to be learned;
- Who encourages practice, practice, and more practice;
- Who confronts inertia by highlighting the role of the victim as a choice;
- Who encourages creative thinking to minimize thinking in absolutes and to maximize choices;
- Who sees mistakes as learning opportunities so that trying new behaviors is less threatening than it could be;
- Who understands that success is measured by what the client has learned to do differently, not by how much has been presented;
- Who values the uniqueness of each client and appreciates how difficult and frightening it can be for people to change.

My goal in counseling is to facilitate the exploration and the journey toward learning so that the client can ultimately move forward without me to meet the challenges and problems of life that can be prepared for only with the acquisition of skills, *not* with preset answers.

> **Facilitate the Process**
>
> **then**
>
> **Get out of the Way!!**

What's it all about for you?

- What values have you held since you were a child?
- Which of these values caused stress for you in your adult life?
- Which of your values is sometimes in conflict with another?
- How do you deal with the inability to rewrite your personal history?
- What satisfies you the most about where you are in your life right now?
- What do you perceive to be your greatest strengths for coping with the ups and downs and the pushes and pulls that life presents?
- What behaviors would you change if you could?
- What would you like your life to be like in the future?
- How are you preparing for your future when life presents so many unpredictable changes?

- Who are the people in your life that have helped with your personal growth the most?
- What did they offer to you that you found particularly helpful?
- What does personal power mean to you?
- How does " . . . justice for all" fit into your counseling philosophy?

Perhaps many of the questions we want to ask of ourselves are the very same questions that we might raise with our clients. Perhaps in most situations the most significant question of all might be, What's it all about for you?

What's it all about for you in your role as counselor?

- How do you define the role of counselor?
- What are the theoretical underpinnings of your counseling style?
- What's the basis for your choice(s)?
- How do you define facilitation?
- How do you justify withholding advice when you're convinced that you know what would solve your client's problem?
- What's the picture you hold as your "ideal self" in your counseling role?

SUMMARY ACTIVITY

1. Take some time to reflect on the questions raised on the preceding few pages. You might even begin to keep an ongoing journal of your responses.

   If you see yourself as I see myself, you will recognize that you are as unique as a counselor as you are unique as an individual. This is not different from the way in which we strive to regard our clients as unique unto themselves. We are each the sum of our particular inherited characteristics and our particular life experiences.
2. With these thoughts in mind, write down and date your answers to the questions that are listed.
3. Keep your responses and review them periodically.
4. Note and thoughtfully evaluate changes that you make.
   - What value do you see in these changes?
   - What new goals will you establish for yourself as you find yourself on a somewhat different personal and/or professional place in your life?
   - What process will you follow to achieve your goals?
   - When will you begin?
5. Take pleasure from each small step that you see as positive growth just as you would encourage your clients to delight in even the smallest successes.

■ ■ ■ ■ ■ ▬▬▬▬▬▬▬▬▬▬▬▬▬▬▬▬▬▬▬▬▬▬▬▬▬

CHAPTER 2

FIRST CONTACT

I've learned so much from my clients over the years and I'm pleased to say that I'm still learning. Most of what I did when I first began counseling was based on what I had learned as a student. Other beginning behaviors were based on my personal assumptions and elements in my own life. Some of what I've learned is that my assumptions are generally reflections of me, and that the view of life that I hold is not necessarily shared by my clients. Therefore, a major responsibility for me is to know my client and my client's view of the world. Every step in the counseling process is important, including the very first contact made with the counselee. What we say and how we say it will set the stage for each counseling session that follows. In this chapter, I'd like us to look at some elements that may be critical to a successful first contact.

It's likely that you will connect with a new client in one of several ways. If you are working at an agency, it is likely that clients will be assigned to you after they have been seen by an intake counselor and some assessment has been made as to the appropriate counselor to be designated for this client. Sometimes the counselor is responsible for the intake interview as well as the ensuing counseling sessions. If you are in a school setting or the corporate world, you may have referrals, walk-ins, or individuals that drop off a message that they would like to see you. If you are seeing clients privately, it will be a phone call from an individual or your call to the prospective client in response to a message left for you. Whatever the case, there is some important work to be done before counseling begins.

AGENCY SETTING

In most agency settings, the client's first contact is with a receptionist who will then direct the caller to an intake counselor. When this has taken place, the clients are either told to contact the assigned counselor or told that they will be contacted by the counselor to set up an initial session. Keep in mind that whether you see value in an intake interview or not, this procedure is required by most agencies and particularly those agencies receiving funding.

Agencies are generally required to report all the quantitative items that one could imagine. This is done for the purposes of accountability and research. Nonetheless, there are some very real questions that might be raised, even about the intake.

- Is all the information supplied by the client accurate? Maybe.
- Is all the information requested relevant to the counseling sessions that will follow? Probably not.
- Is this the best first step in establishing an effective working relationship? Not in my opinion.
- Is this a reality with which we must deal in most agency settings? Yes.
- So now what?

If I am called directly by a potential client, or required by the agency to initiate the counseling procedure, I keep my phone contact as simple and as brief as possible. I introduce myself, check out how I should address the client, check out where I may call if necessary, share my "rules" as governed by the agency, emphasize confidentiality, and make an appointment. I would rather not refer, in any way, to the file of information that I have probably been given by the intake counselor unless I'm asked about it by the client. If asked, I would simply acknowledge its receipt.

I have found that prospective clients sometimes ask if the counselor thinks that they can be helped. My response: That's exactly what we're going to work together to do. I'll see you on _____ at _____ A.M./P.M. My objective in this instance is to lay the groundwork for a facilitative relationship between counselor and client rather than suggesting that I will be providing answers.

Let's look at another possibility. You may be working in an agency where the receptionist refers clients to the counselor who is next in line. In a situation such as this, you may be responsible for the intake interview as well as the counseling sessions that are to follow. This is my least favorite of all possible scenarios because it tends to place the counselor in the role of fact *gatherer* rather than *process facilitator.*

As you may have gathered by now, my goal is to join with my client in working toward the acquisition of new understandings and new skills as opposed to being the authority who prescribes solutions. When I ask all the questions that a form requires and I gather all this information from a client with each question answered, I am likely to become the perceived "authority." Given that this could be the case, I want to do what I can to separate my role of "intake counselor" from my counseling role. To do this, I would sit at my desk to gather the information, and I would inform the client that this is important for the agency so that we can go ahead. When completed, I would leave my desk and, without pen and paper, I would join with my client in my counseling setting and begin the counseling session in my new role. Even one extra chair in the room could do the trick and allow for movement out from behind the desk to make this transition. Now the setting is as it would have been if the intake had been done by someone else.

- Different position
- Different role
- Different style
- Different agenda

When the intake is done by an intake counselor, you then have a critically important decision to make based on the file on your desk and how directive you choose to be.

- Will you read the file?
- Will you attempt to determine the nature of the problem from the information in the file?
- Will you begin your first counseling session by saying something that begins with, "I see from your file that . . . "?

You've already read some of what I've written in this book and, as a result, I imagine that you have at least a rudimentary sense of my approach to counseling. What do you think I would say? What do you think would be the justification for my choice?

- Liz, you gave lots of information about yourself in the intake interview, what do you think is most important for me to know about you?
- Liz, I see from your intake interview that you have five children. That must keep you very busy.
- So, Liz, how shall we begin?

Of the three possibilities that I've given, the one I would unquestionably avoid is the option that deals with Liz's children. The content that it includes may have little or no relevance to her problem. I could be far afield from what has brought her into counseling, and I would be running the risk of imposing the agenda. That would be contrary to my counseling objective.

I can argue in favor of either of the other options that I listed. My argument for the first would be that it acknowledges the time and effort that went into completing the intake and then puts the matter of setting the agenda in the client's court. My opinion of the third option is that it creates an intermission between Act I, the intake, and Act II, the counseling session, with the setting of the agenda clearly up to the client.

My personal choice would be to use the fewest number of words to get us where we need to be. Additionally, I particularly like the manner in which the last option suggests the start of a journey that we will take together.

- What would *you* say?
- What is *your* justification for your choice?

SCHOOL SETTING

In a school setting, there is lots of information that exists regarding students. Demographic information is readily available. Anecdotal information recorded by teachers, administrators, and previous counselors is often also available. This is particularly the case if at issue is a student who has had previous difficulties, whether academic or behavioral in nature. In addition, you will probably have a teacher or administrator who will willingly describe his or her perception of the presenting problem if the student is not self-referred.

Once again, you are faced with the issue of deciding how much you want to know before you meet with the student. What I would want to know are the descriptions of outcomes rather than any labels that may have been attached to this youngster.

- I want to know if he is often truant,
          not
  if he hates coming to school.
- I want to know if she's failing in her classes,
          not
  if she's "just plain lazy."
- I want to know if he gets into fights,
          not
  if he's a constant troublemaker.
- I want to know if what is being reported is a recent change in behavior,
          not
  if this is an incredibly volatile kid.

I will know very quickly what the people in charge perceive as this youngster's problem, or at least I will know what behavior is unacceptable to them as a result of this youngster's problem. It's extremely important to consider the basis of their referral to be the resulting behavior precipitated by something not yet determined. In my view, only the student knows the cause, whether realized or not, and it is the student who can find alternative ways of acting. This is where the counselor comes into play. So here we go!

I would send for students at what I consider to be the least intrusive time in their day. Despite what occurred to prompt the referral, I would greet the student with an attitude of welcome into a new relationship.

> **Counselor:** Hello _____, I'm _____ and I'm pleased that we could meet today.
>
> **Client:** (Anything can happen—total silence, acting out, expressed confusion as to what I might want, and so on)
>
> **Counselor:** (I'm prepared to go on.) I've asked you to come into my office today because several of your teachers are having a problem with ____*(describe behavior)*____ . What's going on?

My objective is to place the presenting problem on the referrer, which is really where I think it belongs, because *they* are having a problem with the behavior. What I'm looking for is the causal factor(s) of the unacceptable behavior, which can lead us to the *client's* problem.

My premise is that something is going on in this young person that is prompting behavior that is unacceptable to the school community. This could be the result of poor decision-making skills, anger, fear, frustration, seeking attention, and so on. I just don't know yet. Therefore, rather than making even "educated guesses," I'm simply going to ask and then explore what the student has to say as together we wend our way toward some awareness of what's behind the behavior.

In my counseling relationship with this student, I will not:

- Debate the student's perception of what happened;
- Ask why the student feels that way;
- Accept "I don't know" as a response;
- Judge any statement by the student as good/bad, right/wrong, or silly;
- Respond to the outcome of the student's chosen behavior with any sarcastic statement, like "You really got yourself in trouble, didn't you?"

What I will do is:

- Ask for the student's perception of events;
- Ask how the student felt when whatever happened;
- Ask what the student remembers thinking at that time;
- Ask what other kinds of events precipitate similar feelings and thoughts;
- Ask what the student was thinking and feeling when the event was over;
- Ask what the "payoff" was for the choice the student made.

When a student self-refers, the situation at hand is hardly different. The only differences that I see are the likelihood that the student will be initially more amenable to the process and that the issues probably have not yet seriously affected the student's performance in school. Therefore, as I conduct the initial interview, my questions are apt to be precisely the same.

I have several goals in mind as I proceed through all of this with the student. Initially, I know that I'm being "checked out" and I want to come through that test in a way that makes it possible for the student to see me as a person who is there to help, not as one more person in his life who might reprimand him. Secondly, I want to understand this person's view of her world, which may be very different from the views of others. Finally, I want to establish a nonthreatening environment for the work we will do at ensuing sessions, which is likely to focus on what the student wants (needs), and how the least negative price can be paid in satisfying those wants (needs). In doing this we will ultimately explore the process of decision making; the reality of the frustration that comes as a result of not having the power to change the rules, beliefs, and behaviors of others; and how to more effectively cope with those things we cannot change.

CORPORATE SETTING

In an industrial or corporate setting, we are dealing with situations that are more similar than they are different from a school setting. The similarities can be identified as "people concerns" such as belonging, recognition, security, accountability to self and others, peer pressure, responsibility, independence, and on and on. Perhaps the greatest difference is that the population with whom we are working has far greater power to choose than students who are not of majority age.

The manner of client referral is also likely to be similar to that in a school setting. Seeing a counselor hired by the company's management can be perceived as being as threatening to the employee as the relationship between the school counselor and the school administrators. Therefore, the counselor's reputation regarding issues of confidentiality is a critical element within each of these organizations. There will be those who will self-refer if they trust the confidentiality of the relationship. There will also be those who will be referred by a manager, supervisor, or employer. The client's job may be on the line in the same way that a student's suspension from school may be the threat. Records of attendance, tardiness, suspected substance abuse, acting out, and poor performance are likely to be as available as they are in a school setting.

Clients' behaviors will also not be particularly different. The rationalizations used by teenagers are virtually indistinguishable from those used by adults. The deficiencies in communication skills and decision-making skills are likely to be the same. If the adults in the business setting were truly effective in these areas, they would not be referred to you nor are they likely to self-refer any more than the successful student.

Are there special circumstances that adults face? Of course there are. However, the question of how different they are from the circumstances of youth remains.

- How different is the pain of loss?
- How different is the fear of change?
- How different are the struggles with authority?
- How different is the anxiety of independence?
- How different is accountability to others?
- How different is valuing one's self?
- How different is wanting to be understood, prized, and loved?

What we as counselors must keep in mind, regardless of whom the client may be, is that the circumstances of life may change as we get older, but the baseline issues of life remain virtually the same. We must, therefore, concentrate on issues rather than particular situations, so that the behavioral changes and learnings that we facilitate are applicable throughout life. Does this mean that school counselors could easily move into the corporate world? In my opinion, the answer is "yes," as long as they are well informed about the aspects unique to this other culture.

PRIVATE PRACTICE

It is my contention that, when new clients call to set up an appointment for an initial counseling session or consultation, my primary responsibilities are to gather specific information, to give specific information, to quickly assess if they are calling for someone with my training, and to establish a date and time to meet. My manner is caring even as it is clearly geared toward the "business" at hand.

Let's look first at whether or not I have the training that this person wants/needs. My experience has been that people sometimes have the notion that they are looking for a psychiatrist when the training from which they might benefit the most might be with a psychologist or counselor. The confusion in the public arena is often no different than whether to choose an optometrist or an ophthalmologist when vision is somewhat blurred. If what I hear in this initial contact suggests pathology rather than the need to develop effective skills, I will immediately recommend another level of training and wish the client well. I regard making this referral as mutually beneficial, professionally moral, and ethically required.

For the appropriate potential client, the "business" of our future relationship is the agenda for this initial contact. I strongly believe that it would be inappropriate for me to participate in a dialogue that would resemble the dynamics of a counseling session. I consider it more professional to stick to "business" because:

- The client and I have not yet agreed to work together;
- I know nothing about the person to whom I'm speaking and, therefore; I have no idea as to the potential impact of what I might say;
- I want to use this time on the phone to inform the client of logistics and parameters relevant to counseling sessions;
- I want to limit our conversation in ways that will get the job done without causing undue anxiety;
- I want to eliminate the need to address business details in our first counseling session.

The following conversation illustrates the kinds of details that can be addressed during the first contact.

Client: I was given your name by _____ and I'd like to make an appointment to come in to see you. My name is Elizabeth _____ .

Counselor: What do you prefer to be called—Elizabeth, Liz, Beth?

Client: Liz is fine.

Counselor: And you may call me Arlene or Dr. King, whatever is comfortable for you. Have you been in counseling before this, Liz?

Client: No, I haven't and I'm really nervous about this.

Counselor: I can understand that. Liz, tell me in a sentence or two what prompts you to seek counseling?

Client: Well, my husband and I just never stop arguing. We really can't seem to agree on how to raise our children. And . . .

Counselor: (interrupting) So there seems to be some real stress in your relationship and some problems communicating effectively. Liz, may I have your address and day and evening phone numbers?

Client: Sure, my address is _____ and my day phone is _____ and my number at home is_____ .

Counselor: May I call you at either of these numbers if necessary?

Client: Please don't call me at home. I haven't told my husband that I'm going to see a counselor.

Counselor: How would you like me to identify myself if I were to call you at work?

Client: Just by name, without the *doctor,* would be fine. Thanks.

Counselor: Let me tell you exactly where my office is and how to get there . . . I also want you to know that my fee is $____ for a fifty-minute session that begins at the time of your appointment, and I require twenty-four hours notice if you need to reschedule or cancel an appointment so I won't have to charge you for your session.

Client: What if there's a sudden snow storm and I can't get there?

Counselor: I would probably call you to reschedule. Surely there can be sudden emergencies that would warrant that exceptions be made. I also want to share with you my professional commitment to confidentiality. You may share anything we talk about with anyone you may choose. I will share with no one unless I believe that you are a serious threat to yourself or another person. Anything else you need to know right now?

Client: No thanks. I've got it all.

Counselor: Liz, I have an opening on Monday at 5:00 P.M. and one at 11:00 A.M. on Thursday. Which would be better for you?

Client: Thursday at 11:00. I'll just take an early lunch hour because I'm close to your office.

Counselor: Fine, I'll see you at 11:00 next Thursday. I look forward to meeting you, Liz. Good-bye.

That initial contact went smoothly, but there are other situations that are more difficult to negotiate.

■ What if a spouse calls on behalf of the partner, or a parent calls on behalf of an adult child, or an adult child calls on behalf of a parent?

I will give all of the business information that I referred to in my illustration but I will *not* set an appointment. What I will do is request that the information be shared and that the prospective client call to set a mutually convenient time for us to meet. I have found that this minimizes broken first appointments and encourages at least a modicum of commitment.

I will also stress that confidentiality is binding for me with the client and, therefore, any questions the caller may have regarding the counseling sessions or the progress being made would have to be asked of the client.

■ What if the potential client is not sure if coming for counseling is the right thing to do or if I'm the right counselor to see?

The best thing I know to do would be to suggest that the person might think about it and call again or they might come in for a consultation with no commitment to continue unless he or she so decides. I know of no benefit to pressuring this person in any way.

■ What if the potential client cannot afford my fee?

I would recommend counseling agencies with sliding fee scales or suggest that the individual could see me every other week if that would help. I'd be really clear that either would be fine.

■ What's the purpose of taking the time to clarify how the client would like to be addressed?

I believe that often it's the little things that convey caring. I sometimes hear assumptions that, for reasons unknown at the time, can be offensive to an individual. Robert may not wish to be called Bob, just as I wish not to be called Arl except by my nearest and dearest people. My point is that just asking for the client's preference can be a step toward formulating a caring relationship. Similarly, offering the client the option of addressing me by title or by my first name can help reduce a sense of perceived distance between us. You determine if you're comfortable with this option when working privately. In schools, agencies, and business settings, it seems most appropriate to me to adhere to the norm of the particular setting in which you are working.

■ What if the potential client doesn't describe the presenting problem in a sentence or two but begins to relate a detailed description?

Interrupt! Interrupt! Interrupt! Without apologizing, I would say that I hear a great many concerns that we can talk about in session and then go right on to the next piece of "business." If we don't interrupt early on, we can be trapped into a counseling session on the phone. Remember that the person you are talking to may be very anxious and not deliberately exploitative of your time. This is a time for you to be in control.

■ What is the reason for questioning where you may call and how to identify yourself?

It's not at all unusual for clients to be secretive about seeking out counseling for themselves. They often don't want coworkers to know and they often don't want family members to know. In my opinion, checking this out right from the start can avoid mistakes and an unintentional violation of confidentiality.

■ What if clients ask how often you will be seeing them and for what duration of time (weeks, months, years)?

I'll answer by indicating that we'll meet once a week unless we agree that more or less often would be better. I'd also say that together we'll determine our success and, thereby, the duration of our relationship.

■ What's the reason for all the "rules" before you even meet the client?

I'll answer this question at first with another question. What's the justification for wasting the client's time with "rules" that could be devoted to counseling rather than business when you meet in session?

What I'm addressing with my "rules" are the boundaries that I have established for my practice. Barring the advent of a critical situation, they are basically nonnegotiable. My reasons for putting them forth right from the start are:

■ To protect my boundaries;
■ To minimize surprises for the client;
■ To model the significance of personal boundaries, which can often be an issue for clients.

- What reasons do I have for not asking for more details such as age, occupation, health, and so forth? My reasons are multiple and open to your argument.

My first point is related to my belief that, in the role of inquisitor, I would be working in an extremely counterproductive way toward the first step of establishing rapport with my future client. In soliciting responses to my questions, I would be systematically placing myself in a position of authority that contradicts my perception of an effective facilitator. Secondly, I cannot imagine that relevant information would not be disclosed as we work through any process of problem solving. It is only at that time that, for the purpose of my better understanding, I might ask for details if they were not forthcoming in the client's "story."

The position that I hold regarding these hypothetical situations is based on what I believe are some of the limits that are related ethically to my role as a counselor. I believe that I do not have the right to know every detail of a client's life if those details are not relevant to the counseling issues. I do not have the right to abuse my role just to satisfy my own curiosity. I believe that too much information too soon can trigger the tendency, shared by many helping professionals, to analyze and conclude that, in their "wisdom," they know what the *real* problem is rather than allowing it to unfold. This, I believe, feeds into a "guru" trap that may cause counselors to become more directive and controlling than they may really want to be. It can also cause counselors to do the work of discovery that clients should be doing.

TERMINATING THE INITIAL CONTACT

The manner in which this first counseling session is terminated is at least as important as the way in which it is begun and proceeds. It will influence the manner in which the counselor is perceived by the client.

The client ordered to seek counseling must continue, but the quality of the initial session will greatly determine the extent to which meaningful work can be accomplished in the future. Obviously, the self-referred client doesn't have to return. Therefore, the quality of the relationship and the initial rapport built in this first encounter is of vital importance.

In my mind, I am never absolutely positive that I can help. In fact, I am absolutely positive about very little, particularly as it relates to human behavior, including my own. I think I have the skills to help. I know I derive satisfaction from being helpful. I will certainly try to help, but I cannot issue guarantees. Therefore, when clients ask, as they often do during an initial session, "Will you be able to help me?," I can only say that I intend to try and I will do my best to help them learn how to help themselves.

I'm reminded of the old riddle:

Question: How many counselors does it take to change a lightbulb?

Answer: Only one, but the lightbulb has to really want to change.

Much like other relationships, the initial contact and first impression can have a lasting impact. You know you're a caring person. Does the client hear caring in your voice? You know you're an empathic person. Does the client feel your empathy for the magnitude of the problem as he or she perceives it? You know that you're a skilled counselor. Can you control the initial contact so it doesn't get away from the "business" at hand, and yet not create perception of you as authoritarian?

To negotiate the first contact skillfully, I believe that you must first believe that it's acceptable to keep it brief and not support what might be a desire for catharsis on the part of your potential client. I strongly vote against gut-wrenching initial contacts. If I were in the client's shoes, I would feel overwhelmingly vulnerable in a relationship I do not yet trust. This possibility suggests that you must skillfully work against what clients new to counseling may think is expected of them.

What information do you want to give to your client? What information do you want from your client? You walk a fine line between how much and too much. You need a plan. That is my commitment as a counselor. My initial goal is to address the factors that have led to the presenting problem. My long-term goals are to facilitate the learning of skills that will enable my client to effectively deal with situations that haven't happened yet, and to learn which situations are best avoided. In essence, I strive to put myself out of business. This may sound incredibly altruistic, but you and I each know that there's another client right around the corner. My position is not based on altruism, but professional commitment to a job I hope will be well done.

SUMMARY ACTIVITY

What you do and how you do it in your initial contact with clients is important. It gets business out of the way and sets the stage for your work together.

1. What is *your* plan?
2. What information do you want from your client?
3. What information do you want to give to your client?
4. How will you establish your first session with each new client?
5. Reread what I've written in this chapter and identify the ideas with which you agree. Discuss with others those points with which you disagree.
6. List *prompt* words for yourself that you wish to remember, and review the list regularly. Keep the list until your plan is so much a part of you that you no longer need to be prompted.

▪ ▪ ▪ ▪ ▪

COUNSELING BEGINS
IN EARNEST

There are many aspects to be considered as we set the stage for effective counseling, ranging from how the counseling room is arranged to the atmosphere that is created in the room. They include what *is* done during each session and what is deliberately *not* done. Most important of all considerations are how we as counselors do what it is that we have studied and practiced, and the manner in which we strive to accomplish our goals as we work with our clients.

THE PHYSICAL SETTING

The environment in which you see your clients is of real importance. It should be pleasant-looking and comfortable with a minimum of visual distractions and outside noises. There should be seating choices that allow clients to choose the distance from you that they wish to establish at any given time. There should be some room to walk about if that's what the client chooses to do. Creature comforts such as a lavatory, drinking water, and tissues should be reasonably accessible. There should be a clock that is visible to both the counselor and the client so that either or both can keep track of time remaining in the session. There should be no barriers between the client and the counselor, except during an intake interview when the counselor is likely to be seated at a desk or table. There should be no telephone in the immediate area and there must be total privacy. Not every work situation will allow for all of these conditions. However, we can strive for the best we can do given the limitations that may be imposed by the setting in which we work. We also need to determine what our priorities are and the extent to which we're willing to "go to bat" for what we consider of greatest importance in the physical setting.

   I consider the issue of privacy to be the most critical of all that I've identified as physical setting "shoulds." Without absolute privacy, the condition of confidentiality is a hoax. If the room is shared, if partial walls separate one counseling area from another, if people can open the door and look in, then the idea of privacy becomes unrealistic. Without privacy, there can be no confidentiality. Without confidentiality there cannot be trust. Without trust there cannot be effective counseling.

Are there limits to confidentiality? There certainly are, and, because they exist, they must be stated openly and clearly to each client at the onset of the counseling relationship. Counselors must be informed of the ethical guidelines for confidentiality as set forth by the American Counseling Association (ACA) as well as the laws that exist within their state. The ACA guidelines and the laws of each state will help counselors prepare and use appropriate disclosure consent forms, which can be the most effective means for understanding the limits to confidentiality for both client and counselor.

Privacy for the purpose of confidentiality brings with it a very serious concern for which I have no answer. We live in a litigious society. Privacy brings with it vulnerability. How do we maintain privacy and yet not be suspected or accused of inappropriate behavior? My thought is that we behave professionally and depend on our reputation among many people to provide us with some semblance of security.

Second only in importance to privacy is the idea that your full attention is the very least that your client deserves. Therefore, receiving phone calls during a counseling session is, in my opinion, out of the question. To take a call, however brief it may be, is not only an interruption to the counseling process, it is also a message to clients that something is of greater value in that moment than they are to you. In this age of answering machines and voice mail, there is really no acceptable reason for taking calls.

NOTE-TAKING

I have heard counselors debate about note-taking since the beginning of my training as a professional counselor. It is something that is likely to be debated long after I am gone from the scene. Therefore, I can only share with you my view on the subject: I am vehemently against the taking of notes during a counseling session.

In the first place, I consider pad and pen in the hands of the counselor a statement of authority. To project authority to the client violates the very essence of the process that I'm advocating in this text. The process that I'm setting forth here is not based on the traditional medical model—in which one party has the questions and the other has the answers—but rather one of partnership. It is the joining together of two or more individuals on a journey of exploration. It is a journey during which the counselor facilitates a process by asking questions that prompt clients to explore, examine, and then determine alternate ways of achieving their desired goals. The answers lie within the clients, not the counselor. The counselor models a process that can be replicated by clients as they learn the way it's done. Therefore, in my opinion, there is no authority present and so there ought not be the presence of authoritative tools like clipboards, writing pads, and writing implements. The partnership is one of counselor facilitation and client discovery that can lead to client awareness, understanding, behavioral change, and, ultimately, to the client's sense of empowerment, skill, and greater ability to effectively facilitate his or her own future.

Secondly, I believe that if you do not remember what you need to remember for the sake of keeping records, you are probably not listening for what you need to know. Beginning counselors too often try to recall the details of what clients are saying. In other words, they try to remember "the story" in which the issues have been presented.

I have serious doubts about the importance of "the story." I believe that the story is the means through which clients present the issues, and it is the issues that are of significance to the counseling that is taking place. Clients may tell you about problems at work. They may tell you about how fearful they are of not meeting the boss's expectations. The same clients may tell you about difficulties dealing with a parent's interference in their relationship with their husband or wife and the way in which they are raising their children.

At first, we might conclude that there are two very important situations that these clients need to address, and, therefore, that it would be important to know and remember the details of the work situation and the details of the relationship with the interfering parent. If we were to arrive at this conclusion, I believe that you and I might be tempted to take notes about each of these situations. I suggest to you that we would then get entangled in one story after another, with the likelihood that neither counselor nor client would remember many specifics when meeting a week later.

In order to identify what is or is not significant in someone's stories, let's ask ourselves some questions.

- What elements of this client's stories are similar to one another?
- What issue seems to be present in both (or several) stories?
- What do we hear this client saying about what needs to be different in order that unhappiness or difficulties can be diminished?

I contend that the client knows the answers to these questions. What we need to do is ask them.

- How do you feel when you interact with your boss?
- What are you thinking when you feel that way?
- How do you feel when you interact with your mother?
- What are you thinking when that happens?
- How would you like to be able to deal with each of these important people in your life if only you thought you could?
- What similarities do *you* see in these two situations?

I believe that the answers to these questions will tell both you and the client that dealing with people in authority is a problem.

Where does that leave us in terms of taking notes? To me it says that I can remember that an agenda item for this client is likely to be issues with authority. You do not need to trust your memory. Write this down after your client leaves. Furthermore, I believe that I can promise you unequivocally that this issue will be presented again and again in different stories and will not be forgotten.

There are also several things you can do to help you remember people, events, and other aspects of a client's stories. Write down the names and roles of significant people that your client has addressed. Write down your impressions, your thoughts, and your feelings. Write down all this and anything else that you consider important, *but* write it all down as soon as you can *after* your client has left, and then review it all *before* your client arrives for the next counseling session. This procedure will give you all you need for reporting purposes (if called for), and all that you need for an intelligent and informed entree into your next meeting with this client.

The point of all this is that there is little, if any, need for you to remember or record each story. It is important for you to listen for the issues and then check with your client to verify that what you think you have heard is, in fact, the essence of what has been said.

> So __(name)__ , it sounds like, whether at work or with your mother, asserting yourself with an "authority" can be a problem for you.

By the way, I prefer to say this with a question in my voice rather than as a statement of *fact*. That is what I consider "checking out" my interpretation. If what I heard is not what was meant, the question in my voice will give the client permission to correct me. If an iota of what I thought I heard was correct, the client will be listening for that permission from me based on the likelihood that I am also being perceived as an authority figure at this early stage in our relationship.

What do you think?

TAPING THE COUNSELING SESSION

There can be some real value in the use of an audiotape recorder for at least some of your counseling sessions. There are also some major considerations to be taken into account before initiating any such process.

The potential values that I see are twofold. The first is the opportunity that the recorded session can give to you, the counselor. It affords the opportunity to critique what you have done in the counseling session. At your leisure, you can listen to the session and thereby determine for yourself what you did that was effective in achieving your counseling goals, which techniques you tried that didn't work as you would have liked, and which opportunities for intervention you missed. Having done this analysis of *your* work, you are then in a position to establish some meaningful behavioral objectives for *yourself* in your next session. There is probably much that you know about potentially effective counseling that you may not yet have fully integrated into your behavior. This can be the very means you need to "tickle" your brain and enhance your professional growth.

The second possible use for a recorded session is for the benefit of the client. This requires giving the tape to the client at the end of the counseling session. I have found this to be especially useful when the client seems unaware of repeated behaviors. I've seen it work effectively with clients that are "yes, but . . . " people and clients who consistently contradict one statement with another statement.

My procedure would be to confront the behaviors in session, give clients the tapes, and ask that they tell me what they think after they've had a chance to hear themselves. I would be using the tape to provide awareness so that we can then work on the client's behavioral changes in session.

One important exception would be the use of tapes with children. Although the child and the parents may agree to the taping process, I am not convinced that it enhances trust and supports their belief in the confidentiality of the counseling process. I have found that parents often have enough concerns about the "family secrets" that their child may be divulging in counseling, and the idea of anyone having such information on tape is more than they want to see happen, even as they may defer to the request based on their perception of the counselor's authority.

When deciding whether or not to use a tape recorder, there are some major considerations to take into account.

- Has adequate trust been established in the client–counselor relationship that taping would not promote additional stress for the client?
- Have you received written consent for the taping?
- Is the client of majority age or is parental consent also required?
- Are you prepared with unobtrusive equipment that will allow for the taping procedure to go on without creating a disturbance or a need for your attention during the counseling session?
- Are you comfortable and do you feel safe that the tape will not be subjected to tampering? (Sad to say, we do live in a litigious society.)

I would consider taping as a viable tool *only* if all these conditions are met. If they are, the process can be very enlightening for either the counselor or the client.

OPENING THE INITIAL COUNSELING SESSION

I greet the client.
I invite the client into the office.
I begin the session.

Greeting the Client

I suggest to you that a step toward establishing a meaningful relationship with your clients begins at the door. The best way I know to acknowledge the uniqueness of the person is to address your clients by name as you greet them and by name as you work through the session with them. Remember that you established in your initial contact how the client wants to be addressed. You cannot presume that nicknames are appropriate. Simple courtesy dictates that we address our clients as they have asked us to be addressed.

Keep in mind that how you present *yourself* also sends a message. Will I be Dr. King, Ms. King, or Arlene King? I will introduce myself as Arlene King, thereby implying to my clients that all options are open to them, except when a first-name basis would contradict the norms of the organization, such as in a school. Once again, I'm striving for some parity in our relationship with one another, but I will not force the issue. The client's comfort is at issue here. I'm comfortable with any of the options, although my preference is to be addressed by my first name, in the same manner that I will be addressing the client. Once again, this reflects my desire to minimize the possible stress that perceived authority might cause in the counselor–client relationship.

Inviting the Client into the Office

I like to take advantage of the time that passes from the door to our seats to begin the warm-up that I believe is important in beginning the session. It's the time for small talk, the vehicle whereby the clients find their voice for the ensuing session. Therefore, rather than statements about the weather or other chitchat, I ask you to consider asking questions that call for more than yes or no responses and are generic in nature, for example, "What do you think of this weather we're having?" *Do not* ask "How are you?" This is a difficult question to avoid because it is ingrained in so many of us as a social gesture, whether we genuinely care or not. Let us hope that, in a counseling relationship, how the client is or how things are going is exactly what we *do* care about. Because it is the main focus of counseling, it does not fit the definition of small talk and is inappropriate to ask in an offhanded manner.

I also would not say, "I'm glad you're here." To me, that is as inappropriate as my dentist saying, when I enter his office with a really bad toothache, he's glad that I'm there, implying that he will relieve my pain, but I could also interpret his statement to mean that he's glad that I'm in pain and had to schedule an appointment.

Beginning with a New Client

Given that we've taken care of "business" over the phone or when we met to set up an appointment for our first session, there is no need to go over any of that unless the client does. My preferred beginning with a new client is to ask, "What would you like to know about me that you don't already know?" My experience has been that clients can ask almost anything, and I answer as briefly as possible so as not to postpone my next question, which is far more relevant to the counseling session. I have been asked if I'm married, if I have children, where I went to school, what my theoretical orientation is, and so on. If I am asked some deep philosophical question, my response is simply that it would just take too long to answer and we need to address what brings the person to counseling.

I end this brief period of getting going by then asking my new client the reverse of my previous question: "What do you think is important for me to know about you?" Now we are on our way.

OPENING SUBSEQUENT SESSIONS

We have finished our chitchat. We've made it to our seats. I look at my client and I say, "So?" That's all I say. I say, "So?" I do *not* say "How did your week go?" That might be irrelevant to what the client wants to address. Nor do I make a directive statement, for example, "Last week you were telling me about your relationship with your father, let's pick up where you left off." Based on what the client has been dealing with or thinking about, that direction from me may also be irrelevant to this moment.

As you read this you might be questioning all the loose pieces that would be left strewn about if I proceed in this way week after week. Let me remind you that I'm listening for issues that we need to address, not the specifics of situations. I also do not need to be the one who ties the pieces together. I will be the one who asks the client how the pieces relate to one another. I see this as modeling a procedure that the client can learn to use: How does this relate to that? What is the common thread in situations that are difficult for me?

When I begin my counseling session by saying "So?," I am opening the door as wide as possible for the client to set the agenda for our session. It is not a flippant question. It is an important question that really invites the client to work, but your tone of voice is critical. You can readily add to the one-word opening if you perceive it to be too easily misunderstood. You might try, "So, where would you like to begin today?" or "So, what do you think we should talk about first today?"

TIME MANAGEMENT

In this day and age, "time" seems to factor into almost everything: get up on time, don't waste time, get there on time, time is money, time runs out, "tide and time wait for no man," time is of the essence, and on and on until the end of time. As in so many other aspects of our lives, time is an important element in counseling. You and the client have established an appointment for a given time. You have a preset amount of time to spend in each session. Your overall counseling goal is to use the time you have with your client in the most effective way possible.

Let's play with this basic issue of time for a while.

- What are the time parameters that you have established with your client?
- What time will you begin the session?
- What time will the session end?
- What difference does it make?

In my view, time management makes lots of difference for me, for the client, and for the quality of the counseling session. Managing time well is important to me because, as a counselor, I want to help clients learn how to take care of themselves psychologically as well as physically. Once again, I want to model that behavior by demonstrating that I take care of myself. I want to know what piece of a day I will be sharing with a client and what piece of that same day I can devote to caring for myself. Therefore, I have established that each of my counseling sessions will be fifty minutes in duration. That is not fifty-five or sixty minutes, any more than it would be forty-five or forty minutes. My selfish reasons are quite basic. I'd like to have some coffee, attend to any physical needs, do some stretches (I get tired of sitting), jot down the few notes I think I want to be sure to remember, and, most of all, I want to clear my head of client "A" so that I can attend completely to client "B." Keep in mind that, during the fifty minute session that I'm working, I'm working hard. I want to take care of myself. I need a break. What about you?

Do clients respect my rather rigid time constraints? Some do and some don't. Some will talk their way right out the door. I'll discuss that later. Managing time well is important for the client. Let's say, for example, that the counseling session is scheduled to begin at 10:00 A.M., and the client arrives at ten past the hour. What do you say? What do you do?

The client may say nothing about being late. That's fine. I, too, will say nothing, but we *will* end at our predetermined time. The client may offer an explanation for the delay. That's fine. We'll use that as chitchat as we move to our seats. I might comment "That can happen," but we *will* end at our predetermined time. The client may apologize for keeping me waiting, and I might indicate that I was concerned, but we *will* end at our predetermined time.

I have several reasons for maintaining my position that are, I believe, on the client's behalf. First, if being late becomes a pattern, then time management may be an issue for this client. This "issue" may be significant in other situations as well, such as arriving at work on time, keeping friends and family waiting when appointments are made, and so on. The "issue" might be one of not having learned the relationship between cause and effect that can have a multitude of implications. By holding to the length of the session that was predetermined, the counseling session becomes forty rather than fifty minutes in this case. Another possible "issue" may be one of planning ahead for possible contingencies (i.e., traffic, construction on the roadway, getting caught by every red light), and accepting that there can be unexpected circumstances that cannot be factored into every situation, and the need to sometimes "roll with the punches."

- Time management
- Cause and Effect
- The Unknown
- Control

The plot thickens.

The Quality of the Counseling Session

I have already said how important I consider a client's sense of safety in the counseling relationship to be. I strongly believe that a preset duration for the session adds to that sense of safety. When we know how much time we have we can use that time in ways that we each believe will serve our needs. A client may choose to maintain a level of small talk in order to avoid dealing with any issue of importance, not because he or she really wants to waste time but perhaps because dealing with "issues" can be scary. This is important for counselors to see, and then counselors should address the avoidance behavior.

A client may come to session with more than one matter of urgency, and then may want to budget the time. I consider this the client's responsibility, so when the client says, "There's something else I want to be sure to talk about today," my response is to say something like, "You lead the way." If the client doesn't bring up the second situation neither do I. To my mind, once again the client is basically in charge, and setting priorities can be an important thing to learn.

Another point that I consider critical to the time parameters and their effect on the counseling session is what I refer to as the client's right to "hit and run." Sometimes clients need to test how it feels to raise an issue that they may never have spoken about before. Sometimes, it's a way of testing for the counselor's reaction. A client can say the unsayable and want to leave it at that. This can only happen if the client has absolute confidence that the session will end on time.

Inasmuch as I've indicated that I consider time constraints to be important, it is surely equally important for me to state who I think is in charge of time. In my view, the counselor has the primary responsibility for time management. The counselor must be prepared to begin the session at the prearranged time, and the counselor is primarily responsible for ending on time. However, the counselor is also responsible for not leaving a client in midstream. This can be avoided by informing the client when only five minutes are left to work. Then, do not allow new material to be introduced at the tail end of a session. This includes the "hit and run" I referred to earlier. My response to new material, whether "hit and run" or not, is: "That sounds important to you and you might want to bring it up again earlier in our next session." Do I bring it up at the next session? I do not. What I do is note whether this is a pattern of behavior. I will comment on the pattern of "hit and run" behavior, not on the specific content of the statement.

> ___name___, at the end of the past few counseling sessions you said some things that sounded really important to you and yet you haven't brought them up again. What's going on?

TIME EFFICIENCY

There is yet another aspect of time that requires examination: the ways in which time is sometimes wasted in counseling sessions.

Every semester in which I have taught the refinement of counseling skills to advanced graduate students, I have assigned the task of transcribing a counseling session with a fellow student. Once this has been done, I ask them to look at each transaction between themselves and their clients and *measure* how many inches of talk they contributed to each transaction. Some students have reported anywhere between three and six inches of counselor talk in a single exchange. If you were to "measure" your talk time, what would it look like? Are you wasting the client's precious time with too many words? Taking the time to formulate your thoughts may truly end up saving time.

> *For consideration:* Over the years of my professional counseling, I have often compared the decreasing of my verbiage to the way I have finally learned to pack more efficiently when I travel. I generally begin my packing by laying out

everything I think I want to take with me, and then I put at least half of it back in the closet. This usually brings me to what I will need. Similarly with the words I use in my counseling sessions. I will say what I need to say, or ask what I need to ask, to facilitate the process. My objective is to eliminate the excess baggage that I hand to my client. Clear and concise statements are most effective. When I say too much, it's usually when I don't know what I'm trying to accomplish. In that case, it may be better for me to say nothing at all.

Then there's the manner in which questions are asked. This, too, deserves your careful attention. It seems that counselors, particularly if they were teachers, and especially if they are parents, have often acquired a style of questioning that seems to include asking the same question in several different ways. I consider this to be another waste of time in a counseling session, especially if your first question is clear and to the point of the issues that were being discussed. For example,

> *Counselor:* What did you mean when you said . . . ? What thoughts were you trying to express? I guess I didn't understand what the point was that you were making. Please explain it.

Perhaps a simple statement would clear things up, for example, "What you meant is not clear to me," or "Tell me more about that."

You can do it!

How about when you ask more than one question at a time? Is this potentially confusing to the client? Probably. In all likelihood, you will end up asking one of these questions again or it will not get answered at all. That would be either a waste of time or a missed opportunity. Ask one clearly stated question at a time.

Another waste of time is the compulsion that many counselors seem to have, talking in complete sentences when a single word inflected as a question can get the work done.

Client: I really hate going to my job every day.
Counselor: Because?

Then there is the failure of the counselor to interrupt and focus on a point the client has made, which allows the client to go on and on until the point gets lost.

> *For Consideration:* Contrary to what many of us were taught as children, interrupting can be a very useful behavior for counselors to employ. It can produce focus on a point that could get lost in storytelling, but it is among the most difficult things for many of us to learn to do. It takes lots of practice to be able to interrupt smoothly and without apologies. However, it can be so significant in

achieving understanding for the counselor and focus for the client that it is well worth the effort required. Try statements like

  (Client's name) , I'm a little confused, what exactly does that mean to you?

  (Client's name) , one second. How does that connect to what you said a moment ago? I'd like to understand better than I do.

Last but not least is the time that is often wasted by counselors who, perhaps, are trying so hard to be effective that they sound like a talking textbook. I'm referring here to the clichés that most of us picked up along the way in our training. Phrases such as "What I hear you saying is . . . ," instead of "you sound angry," "you sound confused," and so on.

For Consideration: Counseling is meant to be a genuine relationship between counselor and client. Part of being genuine is to speak like a person rather than a textbook. This is unlikely to be an overnight change. More likely, it will be a slow and steady progression from stock phrases to authenticity that will require awareness, conscious effort, and lots of practice. We all begin with the textbooks but then we can move on.

The time that might be wasted as a result of the habits illustrated here may, at first glance, seem minuscule and not worth bothering about. However, a few seconds here and there, or a minute or so throughout a session, can waste a significant fraction of the work time available. Time management and time efficiency can make a difference and it can be done. It requires that you examine the work you're doing very carefully. I like to think of it as a part of "smoothing the rough edges." I believe that clients contract for my time and my services. My services are limited only by my skills and the designated time we have together.

Before I talk about ending a session, now might be a good time for you to consider your own answers to the following questions.

What do you think about time constraints for counseling sessions?
What are your thoughts about privacy?
What points have I made with which you take exception?
Because . . . ?
What are your thoughts about taking notes during a counseling session?
How can you provide comfort and safety in your counseling sessions?
What will you do to "smooth some rough edges"?

THE LAST FIVE MINUTES

I consider the last few minutes of every counseling session to be at least as important as any other time during the session. It isn't the time to run out of steam, but it is the period of time in which we "wind down," "wind up," and look at the experience of the counseling session.

First let me explain that as rigid as I am about the length of a counseling session, I am, in contrast, somewhat flexible about how long the "last five minutes" might be. I think that the emotional level of the session should be the determining factor. Not all counseling is fraught with heavy emotional material, quite the contrary. Most sessions revolve around cognitive processes related to decision making, prioritizing, value clarification, communication skills, goal setting, and action plans. Therefore, most sessions require very little of what I refer to as "winding down." However, when emotions are significantly evident, whether rage or sadness or any emotion between these two, time is necessary to help clients reach a level of balance that is safe and reasonably comfortable before they leave. To me, that means facilitating the "winding down" process by moving from the heart to the head, with enough time to get there. By no means do I mean to suggest that clients need necessarily walk out from a session happy. My preference is that they leave with a plan of action that is in their best interest or with few questions and little confusion that have yet to be resolved. My point is that the counselor must time the process so that, whatever the issues may be, the client leaves intact. This could mean that the session "winds down" sooner than five minutes from the end.

Let's look also at the more cognitive session. This is the session when behaviors have been examined, decisions have been made, or skills have been practiced. These are what I am referring to as "wind up" sessions. They call for summarization of what has been covered, what has been learned, and, perhaps, even actions to be taken.

You can easily find text after text that will refer to the counselor's summarization of the counseling session. To the authors of those texts, I say, No! No! No! To my way of thinking, when the counselor summarizes the highlights of the session, it is the same as the classroom teacher who summarizes what has been covered in class. In my opinion, the only material that was actually covered in class was the material that the students learned and took away. Anything not learned was not covered by anyone other than the teacher.

Counseling is not any different. Therefore, for the counselor to summarize the session is as inappropriate as the teacher's summarization. In keeping with this contention, I believe that the most effective way to conclude the counseling session is for the counselor to initiate the summary process and to step aside for the client to do the work. Not only does this method serve to reinforce any realizations or learning, it also provides the counselor with valuable information as to what was *really covered* and what was *really learned* in the session. Nothing else really matters.

This process need not be very complicated nor need it take very long. The counselor is not requesting a line-by-line playback of everything said in the session. The counselor is requesting a synthesis of what was the most meaningful for the client. It might be something like

> _name_ , we have just a few minutes left in our session today. What do you consider to be the most important thing we talked about?
>
> or
>
> What will you take away from today's session that you want to think about?
>
> or
>
> In our session today you said that there were some things you want to do differently. Review your plan for what you said you will do and when you will do it.

Some counselors will also use the "winding-down" time to process the counseling experience with the client with questions, for example, "What was it like to share with me today?" or "What are your concerns and hopes at this point?" I generally choose not to ask questions of this nature at the conclusion of a counseling session. It has been my experience that questions of this kind often reopen, rather than help to close down, the counseling experience for the client, without adequate time left to pursue any vital points. My preference is to open subsequent sessions with these questions if they are particularly relevant to the client's last counseling visit.

There are many possibilities in terms of what you might ask, depending on what transpired during the counseling session. Your client's response will give you important information as to the client's focus and the client's priority for that day. I believe that what the client says was most important is indeed what was most important. I believe that the only action that stands a chance of taking place is what the client commits to doing.

With this in mind, I offer this again for your consideration:

> If the counselor summarizes the session, it is like the teacher summarizing the covered material. If the client summarizes the session, it is like the student stating what has been learned.

How do you want to use the last few minutes of each counseling session?

SUMMARY ACTIVITY

1. First session: Client self-referred.
   a. How do you plan to greet your client?
   b. What do you plan to say to open the session?
2. First session: Client mandated to attend.
   a. How do you plan to greet your client?
      Same as 1. _____   Different than 1. _____   (check one)

If "Different," explain: _____

_____

b. What do you plan to say to open the session?

Same as 1. _____   Different than 1. _____   (check one)

If "Different," explain:_____

_____

3. What differences in behavior do you anticipate from your mandated client as compared to a client who self-referred?

4. How will your approach differ from that which you would use with a "self-referred" client?

5. Will you audiotape the counseling session? For whose use?

6. How will you end the session?

7. Give some thought to establishing *your* counseling format.

Small talk	What will you say?
	What might you ask?
Work time	How will you begin?
	When will you end?
	How will you end?
Conclusion	Who will "process" or summarize the session?
	How will you initiate this activity?

8. Summarize the points that you consider to be most significant in your approach toward a new client.

CHAPTER 4

BASIC COUNSELING PROCEDURES

We employ specific processes to achieve behavioral change. As in any other craft, the tools and the methods that we select are in response to the job to be done. In counseling there are many basic tools and techniques that can accomplish a great deal, and some that are very specific in their purpose. When they are each used as needed they help us provide useful and facilitative counseling. The more we become facile in utilizing them in combination with one another, the better we can provide effective counseling worthy of our profession.

BUILDING TRUST

Woe unto the counselors who advise their clients to trust them. Perhaps I'm unusual, but I tend to be most suspicious of people who tell me to trust them, whether it's the carpenter who advertises his trustworthiness or the therapist who tells me that my trust is important.

We tell our clients that we are ethically bound by rules of confidentiality and, hopefully, our reputation of caring and helpfulness will precede us as we work in the counseling arena. Despite these factors, trust must *develop* in each and every relationship and it is the result of behaviors rather than promises.

Clients will develop trust in you as a result of what you do as well as what you don't do. The demeanor you present, as well as the interest and empathy you impart, will foster trust. The absence of inappropriate laughter, sarcastic remarks, and dismissing expressions or gestures will foster trust. Being on time and not canceling appointments fosters trust. Scheduling appointments for a time of day when you are up to the work of counseling fosters trust. Perhaps last, but surely not least, is the *fact* that you maintain confidentiality regardless of who might call about your client; who the client might choose to invite into a session; where you might meet the client; and with anyone with whom you may process the work you are doing.

Calls from interested parties must be referred back to the client; sharing must be done only by the client if another person is in a session; counselors must take their cues from clients outside of the counseling office; and only procedures, practices, and problems are to be discussed with other professions.

Trust is an important ingredient in any significant relationship. It is critically important if the process of counseling is to be successful. It's important to keep in mind that establishing a trusting relationship is in itself a process and not a point in time. Clients who have experienced broken trusts are apt to test your commitment in various ways. I have known clients who acted out periodically to test whether I would continue to care about them or scold and write them off as others have done in the past. I have known clients who have come up to me at a theater or restaurant to greet me and introduce the person with them. Clearly, this is a time for me to refrain from identifying the individual as my client. I have had clients who have brought a friend, a colleague, or a family member into session to assist them in resolving a conflict. This situation challenges me to reveal nothing that my client has shared with me and only to facilitate their interactions.

SILENCE

The power of silence as a counseling tool can hardly be overstated. It is not what clients expect. Keep in mind that most clients will come to you expecting to get things "fixed." They have not been successful in handling whatever has been troubling them. They may not know what to do or how to do it. They may not even be sure of the "problem." Chances are they have talked to family and they have talked to friends and neither has helped. They have acted on some advice, and they have ignored some advice. Whatever magic they may be seeking, they are expecting it from you.

Deliberately remaining silent is likely to be the one counseling technique that you have practiced the least. It is also at the top of the list of behaviors with which helpful and well-meaning people have the greatest difficulty. You've practiced clarifying, restating, reflecting, and so forth. How much attention have you given to remaining silent? How long is one minute of silence when you're sitting across from someone who is expecting help from you? Try it, and we'll probably agree that it seems like an eternity.

Select someone to act as your client. Sit across from this person as you both remain silent for sixty seconds (on the clock). Maintain eye contact without staring. Express nonverbal interest without appearing to be patronizing or impatient. Do not say a word!

What were your thoughts?
What were you feeling?
When do you remain silent?
What do you do while remaining silent?
What do you think is likely to happen?

My most frequent use of silence is at the start of any counseling session. I have no preset agenda, therefore I have no directions to give or topics to introduce. What I do have is a keen interest in where the client is and where the client wants to go in this session. As I've said in an earlier chapter, I trust that whatever the client introduces will relate at the process level to the issues of importance. Having said this, I will share with you once again my opening line at almost all counseling sessions. Only somewhat facetiously, I will tell you that it took years of too many words to come up with it.

My opening line is "So?" Or, at most, "So, what's happening?" This is accompanied by a pleasant look and direct eye contact with my client. It is followed by as much silence as it takes for the client to respond. If the client repeats my "question," I restate it in a declarative way and sit silently. I do not say this to be "clever" nor do I say it because I'm too lazy to say anything else. I say it because I believe it translates into

> I'm ready to work with you. What we work on is for you to determine. You (client) are in charge of what we do here, and you (client) are responsible for how meaningfully the time is used.

In this particular scenario, I will remain silent for as long as it takes but I will be working to pick up body language signals from my client to which I will respond if the indication seems to be that the client is ready to begin.

> I see you starting to say something and then you stop (my inflection will indicate a question).

Rather than telling you what I think will happen, I'll tell you what has happened in the past.

Client: I'm really uncomfortable sitting here and doing nothing.

Counselor: What would you like to do instead?

Client: Aren't you going to say something?

Counselor: What would you want me to say?

Client: Something. Anything.

Counselor: OK. What would you like to talk about today?

Client: OK. I guess this means I start.

I'm not saying that this is necessarily what you might choose to do to open each counseling session. I am saying that it works effectively for me. So much so that after one or two such beginnings with the same client, the client either responds immediately or initiates the session by saying "so," and then goes on. It sometimes becomes our "little joke."

There is little question about the stress that can be generated when two people sit across from one another with nothing behind which to hide and the question being who will get things going. If counselors begin with anything but a very basic question, like the one I've indicated, they run the risk of imposing an agenda that may not be significant for the client. It isn't what I want to do.

Silence is also useful after asking the client a question. In my supervisory experience, I have seen counselors become uncomfortable when there isn't an immediate response from the client. There seems to be a tendency on the part of many counselors to then question the clarity of what they have asked or perhaps the statement they have made. Then they rush to ask it again or say it again, intending to resolve the confusion.

My hope is that we will be simple and clear in the first place, and, trust that if we have not been understood, the client will say so. The thing for us to do as we maintain our silence is to again watch for visual clues. You can tell when clients are thinking: Look at their eyes. Give them time. Learn your client's style. Is this client someone who generally responds immediately and, perhaps, thinks out loud, or is he or she someone who thinks about the question and then responds? There truly are different styles, There are "internal thinkers" and "external thinkers." I consider it very important that you remain silent and give your clients the time they need.

- Silence does not mean the absence of work.
- Silence is generally difficult to maintain.
- Silence can be an important counseling tool.
- Practice makes silence more tolerable.

I consider it vitally important that we draw a clear distinction between the deliberate use of silence and passive listening. Silence is a tool that we employ to achieve a specific result. In most cases that is to give the lead to the client and to give the client the time necessary to determine the direction in which we will travel. Passive listening, on the other hand, is void of purpose. Taken to the extreme, it will yield storytelling without direction, and generally accomplish little more than the passage of time. It provides no focus, no clarification of issues, no acquisition of skills, and little benefit to the client. It is what a patient friend might offer to someone who says that they "just need to get it off their chest." It truly is not a counseling tool of value.

CATHARSIS

I believe that allowing clients to go on and on with the details of events that have troubled them requires a significantly important judgment on the part of the counselor. Some may consider it rambling without purpose. It may only serve to minimize a high level of anxiety brought by a client to a new relationship. Initially, that might be purpose enough. It could be that so much has been stored by the client that the opportunity to vent it all is the client's uppermost agenda.

Personally, I find it difficult to refrain from interrupting with questions designed to connect this piece of the story with that piece of the story. Difficult or not, that's where the judgment comes into play. My desire to connect pieces, to achieve focus, and to understand may be less important initially than the client's need to "get it out."

How do I know? I find out from the client with a simple statement like, "Sounds like you want me to know all that's been going on for you." The client's response will determine my behavior. Will I continue to refrain from making connections and striving for focus? Only initially, when the story is new and the client appears to be extremely anxious. The "judgment call" is likely to be appropriate when it is based on this simple check with the client. The most effective choice will be for the counselor to allow for venting, when that meets the client's need, or to provide focus for the client who is ready to work beyond catharsis.

LISTENING AND DECODING

Listening without offering meaningful responses will yield little for clients beyond the possible benefit of catharsis. The client who comes to you is likely to be looking for more than that most of the time.

Some counselors I've known have employed a technique of playing back what a client has said as a demonstration of proof that they were listening. I must admit that I find this procedure extremely annoying. It suggests to me an echo chamber that seems extremely one-dimensional. My preference is to work to "decode" the client's words, to hear the thoughts and then to reflect what I think I hear as the feeling that seems to accompany the thought, or to ask the question that may help to expand the client's thoughts, always remaining tentative rather than absolutely conclusive in my statement. For example,

- That sounds like it might be a dilemma for you.
- You seem to be angry about that.
- Sounds like you're really not comfortable with where you are at this point in your relationship.
- Seems as if there's a lot happening in your life right now that isn't very much in your control.
- I'm wondering if that has happened to you before?
- Even though you "got even," you don't sound very satisfied.

A first step in demonstrating effective listening skills is to paraphrase or reframe the statement that you heard. However, if counseling is to be effective, the process needs to move forward, which requires taking steps beyond just listening. It requires decoding the story in order to get to the issues. Simplistic as this may sound, it requires active participation on the part of the counselor. Silence is a powerful tool when used deliberately and appropriately. However, decoding through reflecting and questioning can be an even more effective counseling tool. Passive listening is surely among the least effective counseling behaviors that a counselor can employ. This is not to contradict what I've said about the deliberate use of silence as an effective counseling tool. Rather, it is to reinforce the idea of selectivity as opposed to passivity. I also believe that "parroting" a client's words is potentially insulting.

What I'm working to do is to listen for trends that may shed light on the client's behaviors that may be precipitating difficulties. I'm listening for the client's description of the behaviors of others that seem to trigger discomfort, anger, withdrawal, or defensiveness on the part of the client. I'm listening for the client's use of language: thinking versus feeling statements, absolutes (i.e., *always, never*), generalizations, minimizing, exaggerating, and so forth. I'm listening for all the clues that I might be about to gather about my clients' view of the world, view of themselves, and previous modes of operation. All of this will help me know a little about them and assist me in understanding the problems they bring to counseling.

I believe that these practices are the elements that engender trust. It is highly unlikely that counseling will be effective if the counselor–client relationship is not built on trust.

SUMMARY ACTIVITY

Spend some time thinking about the questions I've listed and then add some questions of your own, for example,

> What will you say to begin each counseling session?
>
> How will you determine the agenda for each session?
>
> How will you achieve a trusting relationship with your client?
>
> What will you do if you meet your client outside a counseling session?
>
> How much silence can you handle?
>
> How long does a minute of silence take?
>
> What will you do while remaining silent?
>
> What is your silence designed to accomplish?
>
> How will you know if you understood what your client meant?
>
> What does *decoding* mean to you?
>
> How will your client's "style" influence the theoretical framework you choose for working with this individual?

■ ■ ■ ■ ■

CHAPTER 5

CRITICAL COUNSELING PROCEDURES

Effective counseling goes far beyond the establishment and maintenance of a safe and trusting relationship. I believe that it is the vehicle for client learning and personal growth. In this context, it requires that the counselor be adept in the use of procedures that will facilitate these processes. Counselors need to know what to ask and how to ask it; how to confront resistance; how to achieve focus when things sometimes seem disjointed; how to challenge without creating a debate; and how to teach decision-making and communication skills without a lectern or a chalkboard.

QUESTIONING

I believe that the counselor who has learned to ask questions effectively is the counselor who will be the most facilitative and who will have the greatest possible impact on client growth and development. Questions are the tools we use to explore, to clarify, to decide, and to plan. The right question can open a new vista for consideration or help to shut the door to an unproductive or unwanted scenario. Perhaps the most important result that can come from the effective use of questions is that it puts the onus of work on the client, which is where it needs to be if long-term learning is to take place. This is no different than the process used by the best educators and the most effective parents.

Rather than providing answers to children's questions, we can ask questions that facilitate the acquisition of skills that will lead to their ability to find answers for themselves. Similarly, rather than answering client's questions, we can facilitate the process of exploration that will teach them to find the answers within themselves.

This is not to suggest that we engage in as absurd an exchange as the following:

Client: What do you think I should do about how unhappy I am in my marriage?

Counselor: What do you think you should do?

Client: If I knew, I wouldn't be here, would I?

41

This client is telling the truth as he knows it and is also saying that he is not being offered much in this counseling exchange. Instead, the counselor might use the client's question as the springboard for teaching problem solving.

Client: What do you think I should do about how unhappy I am at home?

Counselor: Let's begin by identifying specifically what is going on that leads to your unhappiness.

This exchange gives focus to the session and simultaneously illustrates that we need to examine contributing factors before we can begin to understand and/or possibly change the effect. The effect (unhappiness) is too big, too nebulous, and, therefore, too overwhelming.

This reminds me of the client I knew who wanted more order in her environment and chose to begin concretely by getting her home in order. She found that she was unable to get started due to the magnitude of the physical mess. She could only begin by relinquishing the idea of "cleaning the house" and replacing it with a list of rooms to be tackled one at a time.

Question: How does cleaning one's house relate to an unhappy relationship?

My Conclusion: No one can clean a whole house. You can only clean one room at a time. No one can eliminate unhappiness except by addressing one element at a time.

Clients often come to counseling seeking advice. This, I believe, is the result of many experiences that have fostered this expectation. Well-meaning friends often give advice. Parents and other relatives are often willing to share their life experiences by giving advice. We pay financial advisors, doctors, lawyers, and accountants for their advice. Teachers give advice that also is well intentioned, but can sometimes sound very much like a threat (i.e., I strongly advise you to get that report to me on time). In addition, most students I have known in counselor training programs have said that they've been advised by many to go into the counseling profession because they are good listeners and give good advice.

Every dictionary definition that I have found repeatedly used the word *advice* in defining *counseling* except when referring to psychological counseling. In this arena the reference is to a *process* aimed at the resolution of conflicts and personal problems. I consider this to be an extremely important distinction.

At the beginning of every February of every calendar year, I call my accountant for an appointment in March. Every March I bring to my accountant all the facts and figures related to my earnings and expenditures from the previous year. He then applies his expertise in tax accounting to my information and we file my taxes. Based on that same expertise, he then *advises* me as to what I should do differently in this year so that I can pay less in taxes and have more tax-free investments. I arrange for my advisement session with him every year. Every year I have different earnings and different expenses. Most important of all, tax laws change from year to year, and it's his job to know of the changes and advise me of the implications those changes will have on my financial goals. He's the expert. Therefore, more often than not, I follow his advice. If his advice doesn't work out as he said it would, I hold him responsible and I'm disappointed.

This is the antithesis of psychological counseling. In psychological counseling we are addressing the dynamics of our lives. We're dealing with choices, relationships, and personal growth. We're dealing with birth and death and every day between them. We're dealing with the quality of our lives as well as the crisis situations that may randomly come our way. We're dealing with the questions that are asked of us and the questions we ask of ourselves.

Some people have had positive influences in their journey through life that have fostered their development of the skills required to minimize dissonance and resolve problems effectively. Some people have developed an apathetic view of life based on their experiences. As they endure the bumps and bruises along the way, they may consider themselves powerless to change things and, as a result, they may become powerless.

Then there are the people who are discontent, in emotional pain, or who want more for themselves. These are the people who will seek counseling. These are the people who are, in my opinion, asking us to teach them what they haven't yet learned. These are our clients. These are the people for whom we become the models from whom they can learn how to facilitate self-counseling. As a result, and unlike my annual sessions with my accountant, they will ultimately leave counseling with tools for more effective living. They will not need to return year after year.

The effective use of questions in counseling is a vital tool in this process. The client in the earlier dialogue really does know what to do about his unhappiness. He just hasn't learned the process for figuring it out and the motivation to implement the process. We teach the process by asking questions. What are the questions? The most essential ones begin with *what* or *how,* to which we sometimes add *when* or *where.* We can also judiciously use *and, or,* or *so* to suggest questions, cautiously use *because,* and forget about asking why.

If I were to be limited to the use of only two words as a counselor, I would want those words to be *what* and *how.* I consider them to be key to the exploration of an issue, to the potential resolution of a problem, to effective decision making, and to more effective communication. The following questions illustrate how useful these two words can be during counseling.

What is going on for you now?
How do you feel about what is happening?
If you knew how, what would you change?

How could that possibly be done?
What difference do you think that would make for you?
What stands in the way of your doing that?
What might the results be?
What else could possibly be done?
How do you feel when you consider that possibility?
What effect do you think that might have on other people in your life?
How do you feel about that?
What's the worst that could happen?
How could you handle that?
What might happen if you said that?
What happens when you use that tone of voice?
How could you have said it differently?
What was the reaction to what you said?
What impact did that have on you?
What were you thinking when you felt that way?
What would your action plan look like?
What might prevent you from expediting your plan?
What if you choose to do nothing?

These questions are just some possibilities. If I were to add *when* and *where* to my counseling language, I could continue with questions such as

When does that happen?
When will you begin to act on your plan?
Where will you do it?

With the use of the inflection of my voice, I can turn *and, or,* and *so* into questions that request additional information with the advantage of continuing the flow with very little counselor talk. I believe that, with this extremely limited repertoire of words, we can provide the client with a great deal of help. We are facilitating a process of exploration while simultaneously modeling how effectively *what* and *how* questions can enhance the decision-making process. Ultimately, clients will be asking themselves the same questions, and some significant counseling will have occurred. This is especially true if we highlight "doing nothing" as a viable option. It is likely that doing nothing has been the chosen option for many clients until now. I believe that we *must* help clients realize that they are responsible for that choice. Doing nothing is hardly passive. *Doing nothing is an active choice with real consequences.*

Now, what about my recommendation to eliminate *why* questions? Consider what *why* questions are likely to yield, if I ask a client, "Why did you do that?"

I don't know.
I've always done it that way.

He made me do it.
Because I felt like it.
Why not?

Often clients are genuinely unaware of why they behave in a particular way. It is not our mission in counseling to provide psychoanalysis, and we are usually inadequately trained to do so. Without proper training, we may be too quick to project our own meanings onto others in a weak and unskilled attempt at analysis. Furthermore, I believe that the why of an action can not only be answered through analysis, it can be uncovered through behavioral change as well. I base this conclusion on my personal experience and the experiences I have witnessed with many clients over the years. What I've seen is that, once we have broken the hold of whatever force has dictated some of our responses, we often are then free enough to recognize its root. Oftentimes, it is just too frightening to accept intellectually that which controls us emotionally. So, perhaps beyond analysis, there may be another route to understanding why without directly addressing the question.

Training aside, I believe the use of *why* questions is generally unproductive in helping us foster behavioral change. This would be particularly true with a limited number of counseling sessions. Another important argument against the employment of *why* questions is that the question is often heard as a challenge; therefore, what is triggered can be a very defensive response. Another factor that would be to no avail.

I also suggested that we use *because* questions with caution. Even as our intent may be to shortcut a question requesting more detail between us, I hear it as *why* in disguise. Comparable to this would be "What made you do that?," which is also a *why* question in disguise. The chances are good that you will get the same response as you would have if you asked *why* straight out.

There are also the *why* questions that incorporate the counselor's advice. For example, if I asked someone "Why don't you try . . . ?," some possible responses are

I don't know how.
I don't want to.
I don't know what will happen.
I've never done that before.
I just couldn't.

There are some questions that also disguise the *why* and include advice:

Have you considered . . . ?
What if you tried . . . ?

Even though these responses could provide easy and additional help from the counselor, it seems to me that the counselor is *rescuing* the client from the work to be done. What might follow could be gratitude from a client who has been shown a better way to deal with a situation, but implied is, "You (client) were not capable of discovering this for yourself and you couldn't have done it without me (counselor)." This doesn't work for me. It saves time, but provides very little learning and very little sense of achievement for the client.

Asking questions that require only a yes or no answer is generally nonproductive, and the responses, even if truthful, are not informative.

> **Counselor:**   Does that make you angry?
>
> **Client:**   No.

What and *how* questions, in contrast, introduce open-ended questions. They invite the client to think, to focus, and to participate beyond single-word responses. In addition, their use can eliminate guessing games by the counselor.

> **Counselor:**   How do you feel when that happens?
>
> **Client:**   I feel really hurt, and sometimes I just want to run away.

On the other hand, the counselor may have been effective in using open-ended questions, and still might create a problem if the exchange had been presented as follows.

> **Counselor:**   What do you think and feel when that happens?

What's the problem here? The counselor has asked two important questions packaged as one. This is potentially confusing; it undermines the distinction between thoughts and feelings that is vitally important in effective counseling. It's also likely that the counselor will have to ask one of the two questions again. It works more effectively when we ask only one question at a time.

In my discussion about the significance of open-ended questions in counseling, I don't mean to suggest that closed questions have no place. However, I see the purpose of closed questions as seeking a simple piece of information.

Sometimes a question isn't called for at all, whether open-ended or closed, and even an open-ended question should have some boundaries. Compare how information about a client's parents is requested in the first four questions to the fifth.

> **Counselor:**   How often do you visit your parents? (How important is the frequency of visits to this issue?)
>
> **Counselor:**   Do you visit your parents often? (Yes or no, then what?)
>
> **Counselor:**   Would you tell me about your relationship with your parents? (This is a direction dressed up as a question.)

Counselor: Tell me about your relationship with your parents. (Not a question. A totally unstructured request that opens all doors.)

Counselor: What do you want me to know about your relationship with your parents? (An open-ended question that suggests boundaries of relevance to the issues of counseling.)

One last point about open-ended versus closed questions. The use of open-ended questions is often most time efficient even though it might not seem so on the surface. Often one closed question leads to another closed question, which may eventually lead to the open-ended question that could have been asked in the first place. Perhaps the following exchange sounds familiar.

A: Do you want pasta for dinner?

B: I don't think so.

A: Do you want something cold?

B: Probably not.

A: Should we send out for something?

B: Again?

A: What *do* you want for dinner?

Once again, my suggestion is to ask the question to which you want an answer and you can avoid guessing games and, perhaps, even avoid annoyance.

FOCUSING

"Focus" gives direction and purpose to each counseling session. It is the means we use to draw the issue(s) out of the details and contradictions that exist in the story told by the client. Often the lack of focus makes situations seem huge and insoluable. Without focus, meaningful counseling cannot take place. There would be a little of this and a little of that, resulting in very little of significance being accomplished. There can be no useful plan of action and no meaningful behavioral change without focus. As a result, counseling can move along as bits and pieces that never quite add up to a whole.

Clients have stories to tell and situations to describe. Sometimes this results in rambling from one episode to another with no obvious connection between them. Furthermore, it often results in the client's perception of the existence of many problems when, in fact, that may not be the case. What do you do when topics seem unrelated? You *ask* the client for the connections.

Consider the difference in focus between the first question and the second one.

> **Counselor:**   You told me about some of your difficulties at work and you're telling me about difficulties at home. How do these situations connect?
>
> **Client:**   I guess it's just that I get so angry at a lot of little things no matter where I am.

or

> **Counselor:**   You told me about how angry you get at work and how angry you often get at home. What's going on in each of these places when that happens?

Using focused questions such as the second one can move the client from storytelling to identifying and focusing on the "problem." Perhaps, in this case, the client may recognize that in both situations she does what others ask of her even when she considers their requests unreasonable. Perhaps it is her general compliancy that is causing the anger. Perhaps that isn't it at all. How will you know? If you ask, you can both begin to focus on the *real* issue.

What if the client's detailed story seems to be unending? You interrupt! It is not in the client's best interest for the counselor to be passive in a situation like this. You can interrupt without being rude and without apologizing for the interruption. I know how difficult this can be due to the upbringing that so many of us have experienced. I am not promoting interruption for the sake of the counselor. The intent is not to take the focus away from the client. Quite the contrary. The interruption is for the purpose of facilitating focus on an issue rather than allowing rambling and unnecessary details to continue.

> **Client:**   She always gives me the same answer and . . .
>
> **Counselor:**   You said, "the same answer"? (implied question indicated by inflection)
>
> **Client:**   Yeah. I ask her if she walked the dog and she tells me to do it myself. Anytime I ask if she's done something, she gets an attitude.

By interrupting, the counselor may well have saved lots of time getting to some issues in a relationship that is in trouble. Perhaps this relationship is in difficulty due to ongoing assumptions? Perhaps ineffective communication is the issue. Perhaps the hostility is the sign of an underlying issue that has little or nothing to do with the questions the client is asking. Whatever the case, it is only through interrupting for clarification that a step can be taken toward identification of the problem and promoting focus on the issue.

Interrupting a rambling client and asking questions that help to focus on issues are surely important counseling procedures that should not be overlooked. However, there is another aspect of focusing that too often is not adequately addressed: Who is the client? The obvious answer is that the person (or persons) with whom you're working is the client. Well, maybe or maybe not. I think it depends on how the counselor conducts the session and the extent to which the appropriate focus is placed on the "client."

Earlier in this text, I made reference to the frequency with which individuals come into counseling with the hope of changing someone else's behavior. Wives want husbands to change. Husbands want wives to change, and so it goes. Clients cannot affect the behavior of others until the counselor focuses the counseling sessions on the existing client. I believe that this is a vital point that sometimes seems to get lost.

> **Client:** He promises to spend time with the kids but never gets around to it.
>
> **Counselor:** How do you feel when that happens?
>
> **Client:** I get very angry and I tell him what a lousy father I think he is.
>
> **Counselor:** You sound really upset with his behavior. I'm wondering what you might be able to do to help change things.
>
> **Client:** What *I* can do?
>
> **Counselor:** Yes, so that you won't be angry so much of the time.

There are many possibilities that could come from this now that the focus is on the work that can be done. She might assume some of his household responsibilities or hire someone else to do them. She might initiate a discussion with him that could result in a specific plan for doing things individually with the children. She might discover in discussion with him that they have overextended themselves financially and that some better budgeting might give him a sense of more freedom to spend time with the children. Who knows what might be the result if only the counselor would address *her* anger, *her* method of communicating with her husband, and *her* action plan for getting more of what she wants in this family. If the focus is on *her*, we might even discover that she is also talking about *her* relationship with her husband. We cannot know the answers in advance, but, if we help to focus on the client, we are more likely to help her deal with the real issues in a productive way.

In one-to-one counseling, the focus must be on what the client does or does not do. The behavior of the "other" must be regarded as a given factor that *may* change, but only if the client's behavior changes. Therefore, the focus of counseling should be on the client's behavior, which may precipitate the unwanted response from the other, and/or the client's behavior in response to the other. You cannot work with someone who is not present in the session. You can only work to change that person's environment by focusing on your client's behavior. I have read transcripts of countless counseling sessions that have gone nowhere when both client and counselor have focused on an absentee's behavior.

An additional factor, relevant to focusing on the client, is the extent to which this process places the power to change things in the client's hands. It mitigates against the victim role and brings the client into a proactive role. This shift in focus will surely influence the client's sense of self and promote behavioral change that can be in the client's perceived best interest.

On the other hand, when working with a couple who have come to you to address their relationship, I believe that there are actually *three* clients present, *the couple plus the relationship.* This may sound more complex than one-to-one counseling, but, in fact, it may be considerably easier to work with effectively. The primary focus is then on the relationship, and you have the advantage of having both contributing elements present.

Similarly, in a family setting, the family dynamic becomes the client and all members of the family are the contributing components to the work. The bottom line in all of this is that, if the focus is anywhere but on the client who is present, the desired changes are likely not to be achieved and, therefore, both client and counselor are spinning their wheels.

CONFRONTING

Perhaps because the media often speaks of confrontations between rivaling countries or combative politicians, too often the use of the word *confrontation* in a counseling milieu seems to cause some counselors to retreat and run away. On the other hand, I have known counselors who will verbally confront clients with a tone that does, indeed, suggest that "the war is on," with the intent of getting the client to "get it right." I have no argument with either group's definition of the word. My disagreement is with the particular definition of *confrontation* they have chosen and the efficacy of their responses.

The most useful definition of *confrontation* that I know speaks of coming face-to-face with differing views, different behaviors, confusion, and contradictions. This interpretation of the word can then provide us with a significantly useful and effective counseling procedure. Let's look at the possibilities inherent in several illustrative confrontations between a client and counselor.

Differing Views

The first exchange illustrates how differing views in a situation, both perhaps valid, can be highlighted when using direct confrontation.

> **Client:**   I just don't know what to do. I get home from a tough day at school and my part-time job, and I barely get into the house when my mother is all over me with a million questions and a list of things she wants me to do. All I want is some peace and quiet for a little while. It's the same thing day after day.

Counselor: Sounds like you want a little unwinding time. What do you think *she* wants?

Client: Who knows what she wants, except for me to fix everything that bothers *her?*

Counselor: Maybe we need to first clarify exactly what you mean when you say you want "a little peace and quiet," and then how you can find out exactly what she's asking for when you get home. Then we can look at ways to fit the pieces together.

The confrontation that I see here is one of accepting the problem face-to-face, and then demonstrating an approach to problem solving. I see this process as validating the client's distress and providing a planned approach to a possible resolution. It seems likely that there is a lot going on here and, by confronting the specifics of what the client has presented together, we can get closer to the real issues involved.

If, however, the counselor does not use confrontation, the possibilities at the start are virtually limitless.

1. He's angry that she hasn't gone back to work since his parents divorced and, as a result, there are financial burdens that are on his shoulders.
2. He sees himself as "the man of the house," with all the chores that go with the title.
3. He perceives his mother's concerns as focusing only on herself and his younger sisters.
4. He's jealous that his sisters have lots of playtime and his life seems like one big drag.
5. He takes orders from his teachers and orders at the job all day, and bristles at what he hears as orders from his mother.
6. He's upset that he was thrown off the team at school because his grades went down.

And so on. Without confrontation at this point, the issues, and their possible resolution, remain unaddressed.

Different Behaviors

Confronting discrepancies between what clients are saying and what they are doing can assist them in getting to know where they truly are in a given situation.

- The client who smiles when telling you how angry he is—what's going on?
- The client who fidgets when telling you that she is fine—what's going on?
- The client who develops a plan for behavioral change and does not follow through—what got in the way? What is the payoff for not changing?

In the case of behaviors and statements that are not in sync with each other, my preference is to confront the inconsistency with an observation rather than a challenging question. I would choose the observation rather than the question because I have found that, in most cases, the client is totally unaware of the discrepancy. Only after awareness can the client begin to examine what is going on. The disparity between what the client is saying and what the client is showing becomes a red flag that suggests to me that something might be going on that we have yet to uncover. However, a word of caution: I believe that we must be careful not to arrive at our own interpretation of what the issue must be. Cultural differences may impact significantly on a client's behavior in counseling. Client's actions may also be the result of any number of possible issues. Fidgeting, for example, doesn't always mean that the accompanying statement is less than truthful. After all, it could mean that the client's slacks are too tight. Smiling doesn't necessarily mean that the client isn't angry. It may mean that the client is uncomfortable talking about anger. Once again, my preference is to trust that the client has the answer to what is going on, if only I will allow that to unfold by merely stating my observation.

Clients who do not follow through with plans for behavioral changes that they have developed might be telling us that something in the counseling process that produced the plan went unaddressed. This can happen. It can mean that the counselor did not pick up on an issue the client set forth, or it might very well mean that the "issue" did not come forth until the client tried to put the plan into practice. Whatever the basis for the omission, the situation is now available and must be addressed or progress will be obstructed.

> **Client:** I just didn't get to put my plan into action this week.
>
> **Counselor:** What got in your way?
>
> **Client:** The opportunity just didn't present itself.
>
> **Counselor:** What might you have done to create an opportunity?
>
> **Client:** Well I guess I could have. . . .
>
> or
>
> **Client:** I'll just have to wait for the right time.
>
> **Counselor:** Or perhaps you'd rather modify the plan.
>
> **Client:** Why wouldn't I do what I said I would do?
>
> **Counselor:** I don't know. What do you think?
>
> **Client:** It does scare me a little.
>
> **Counselor:** What about it scares you?

Now we're going where we need to be whether or not we have been there before. No judgments, no cajoling, just further exploration toward resolution through confrontation.

Confusion

Client: Everything in my life is just one big mess. You know what I mean. Just a mess!

Counselor: No I really *don't* know exactly what you mean. Tell me.

This simple example is intended to illustrate that it is the *counselor's confusion* that becomes the counseling means designed to help the client confront his lack of clarity and specificity in his statement. Furthermore, by confronting the client's generalization, we can avoid projecting what we would define as "one big mess" and, thereby, resist the temptation to assume what is not yet known. This isn't complicated and it isn't a ploy. It is a genuine statement of confusion, because we really do not *know* what was meant by the client's statement.

Contradictions

Client: I had a terrific week at work and I've decided that my job is really not a problem. Isn't that great?

Counselor: What was different for you at work this week?

Client: Oh, I don't know. It's just that there weren't a lot of arguments, and my supervisor wasn't constantly on my case for every little thing.

Counselor: I'm wondering what *you* did differently at work this week.

I guess that because I believe strongly in the relationship between cause and effect, and because I also believe that rarely, if ever, does the dynamic of an ongoing environment change of its own accord, something the client did or did not do was likely to be different. I see my first task in this scenario to be confronting the reported change in the client's viewpoint, and then promoting the concept that, when the client changes her behavior, the behavior of others may change as a result.

In my experience, the contradictions rarely surface in a single counseling session. More likely, a client will say one thing one week and then may say something quite the opposite at another time. This can then create a situation that becomes a blending of confusion and contradiction.

Client: I had a terrific weekend. I got to see the movie I wanted to see, and I also got to visit with my parents for a while.

Counselor: I'm a little confused. I think you've told me in the past that you dread visiting with your folks because of all the bickering that goes on there.

Client: Yeah, but this time I decided not to let it bother me.

Counselor: How did you do that?

Client: First of all, I made up my mind that I was leaving in an hour and I told them I could only stay that long. I also decided that I wasn't going to get involved with their nonsense, so I just took the stage and told them all about my classes at school.

Counselor: So, you went in with a plan for yourself.

Client: I sure did and I made myself stick to it.

Counselor: How did you do that?

Client: I kept telling myself that I can handle an hour and what they do between themselves is not my problem.

Counselor: You carried out your plan for how *you* would behave.

Client: Yeah, and it really worked.

Counselor: Sounds like you made it work.

My objective in this example is to demonstrate that the counselor's genuine confusion and the client's contradictions call for confrontation. If the counselor chooses not to work with these circumstances, the end result can be a lot of talk that goes nowhere. Then counselor and client end up with a meaningless and nonproductive session.

Tidbits for Consideration

Check out the different examples here and see if you agree with my view of which approach is likely to be most productive.

Differing Views and Behaviors

Client: I'm really sick and tired of coming home to a hassle every day.

Counselor: Sounds like coming home is not a happy time for you. (No progress)

versus

Client: I'm really sick and tired of coming home to a hassle every day.

Counselor: What do you mean? (Counseling begins)

Confusion

Client: I just want to be happy.

Counselor: I'm sure you do. (No progress)

versus

Client: I just want to be happy.

Counselor: What do you mean? (Counseling begins)

Client: You know, just not being so down in the dumps all the time.

Counselor: What specifically would be different if you were happy?

Client: I guess I'd be a lot happier if everyone wasn't taking advantage of me.

Counselor: Everyone?

Client: My parents, my boss, my husband, the kids . . . everyone.

Counselor: Pick one __name__ , and tell me what happens.

Contradiction

Client: A friend of mine went back to work last month, and she was telling me how good it feels to have some money that doesn't always go toward paying regular bills.

Counselor: Extra money sounds good. (No progress)

versus

Client: A friend of mine went back to work last month, and she was telling me how good it feels to have some money that doesn't always go toward paying regular bills.

Counselor: How does making extra money fit with what you've said about how you like being home with your children and involved in their activities at school? (Counseling begins)

While counselors should keep in mind that clients have the right to not change their behavior, it is our responsibility to confront that choice.

Client: This plan that I came up with sounded good, but doing it is really hard work. It gives me a headache when I have to keep thinking so hard all the time.

Counselor: So, just not bothering would be a lot easier for you.

Client: It sure would be, even though it would still be the same old stuff.

Counselor: Sounds like you have a tough choice to make.

Client: I know I should do the work but . . .

Counselor: (interrupting) You really don't have to.

Client: But then I'm right back where I started.

Counselor: That's really up to you.

It really is the client's choice, isn't it? To not change behaviors is a real option. The counselor's responsibility is to confront the choice so that the clients can be very clear about their responsibility to themselves about the outcome.

Confrontation need not be a battle. Rather, it can be a means by which we facilitate our clients' exploration of their own thoughts. Through our expression of confusion, we can assist their movement toward clarification. It can be the way in which we help them sharpen their own listening skills so that they become better aware of contradictions in their attitudes and behaviors. Furthermore, through the questions we ask in seeking clarification, we can promote an awareness in our clients of the information they may be lacking.

At this juncture, a procedure that has often worked for me has been to encourage imagery. I ask clients to imagine the ideal "picture" for their given situation, and then I ask questions that encourage them to compare that ideal to what they are experiencing in their life.

What looks different?
What parts of the picture are givens?
What changes could be made?
What fantasies could possibly become realities?
What would you have to do to make those changes?
What would be the gains for you?
What if you could change only some things?

Imagining a better picture and recognizing that changing the current situation to a picture that is better, though not necessarily the ideal, can be highly motivating for some clients. I have found that this technique works best with clients who are seeking improvement rather than those who may be driven by the pull of perfection.

The combination of effective questioning, focusing, and confrontation is the best way I know of addressing client resistance to either the counseling process or to change itself. Consider the questions that I have listed as examples of possible ways in which you might confront a stuck or resisting client.

- The mandated client who sits silently hostile:
  - How would *you* like to use the time we must spend together?
  - What will *you* get out of our time together if we just sit out the clock?
  - You seem to be very clear about what you want to do here. How do you see that helping the situation you're in?

- The adult or child who appears nervous or intimidated by the counseling situation:
  - What would you like me to know about you, because we're meeting for the first time?
  - What would you like to know about what counseling is?

- The couple or family in which only one person does the talking:
  - What's your reaction to what name has been saying?
  - What has name left out that *you* think is important?
  - I think I have a clear picture of how name sees the situation. What's your picture of what's been happening?

If we accept confrontation as a process of coming face-to-face with discrepancies, choices, confusion, and resistance, we can incorporate it as a valuable time-saving tool in counseling, and help educate our clients to use it as a meaningful way of modifying some negative thought processes, enhancing relationships, and taking responsibility for themselves. Confrontation can be a valuable tool rather than a threat.

SUMMARY ACTIVITY

1. Deliberately ask *why* questions of your friends and family members. Evaluate the responses you get.
2. Practice replacing *why* questions with *what* and *how* questions. Evaluate these responses. What differences do *you* find?
3. Questions for your consideration:
   - How will you help your client focus on issues when story details don't seem to connect?
   - How will you deal with discrepancies and contradictions in what your client says?
   - How will you approach the client who is resistant to behavioral change?
   - How will you *challenge* your client into action?
   - What does having "no choice" mean to you?
   - What are "open-ended" questions?
   - When would it be useful to ask a "closed" question?
   - What are some questions you might ask to facilitate the counseling process?
   - What, in fact, is your view of "the process"?

■ ■ ■ ■ ■ ▬▬▬▬▬▬▬▬▬▬▬▬▬▬▬▬▬▬▬▬

CHAPTER 6

LIFETIME TOOLS TO TEACH

The counseling relationship affords us the opportunity to employ tools that will not only help to resolve immediate concerns, but will also provide our clients with tools they can use in the future. Sometimes I wonder if one is more valuable than the other. I most often conclude that, if we do our job effectively, our clients will win on both counts. In my view, effective decision-making skills and effective communication skills are the two most essential tools for effective living.

DECISION MAKING

Every individual whom you will work with in your counseling practice will have had years and years of experience making decisions. From the moment we open our eyes in the morning and decide whether to get out of bed, roll over, or to hit the snooze alarm, until we return to bed at the end of our day and decide whether to use a pillow or not, we are each making decision after decision after decision.

Some of our decisions have a relatively neutral impact on our lives and our environment. Other decisions that we make can have some degree of insignificant to highly significant negative or positive effect on us. As with any absolute, few people are likely to achieve completely positive results all of the time. However, it may be that for some the negatives are of minimal significance, short term, or readily correctable. These are the people who have learned the skills of effective decision making whether they realize it or not. They may have so thoroughly integrated the process that they have no need to guide themselves through it step-by-step. It has been learned.

Then there are those individuals who seem to end up with negative results more often than not, yielding more significantly negative impact on their lives than they can reasonably accept. These are the people we can help to learn more effective decision-making skills. This learning, as with other skills, can yield a sense of personal power and chip away at what might have become "a loser mentality."

I'll lay out the decision-making process and then I will restate it in the way in which I prefer to present it in a counseling relationship.

DECISION-MAKING PROCESS

1. Awareness of dissonance
2. Statement of the problem
3. Gathering of possible solutions to the problem
4. Examination of possible consequences (both negative *and* positive) for each possible solution
5. Selection of the alternative that seems most apt to solve the problem
6. Acting on the selected alternative
7. Evaluation of the outcome

RESTATED DECISION-MAKING PROCESS

1. Awareness of discomfort, annoyance, dissatisfaction, uncertainty, etc.
2. Question: What is it that you think you want?
3. Question: What are ways in which you might get what you want?
4. Question: What is each alternative likely to cost you?
5. Question: To what extent are you willing to pay the price?
6. Question: What is your plan?
7. Question: How will you measure the effect of your choice?
8. Question: What will you do if you're not satisfied with the results.

Let's look at each step along the way in the restated decision-making process.

1. There is no call for problem solving and no inclination to solve a problem unless there is an awareness of the existence of a problem. This may seem absurd at first reading, but think about it! We often *feel* the existence of a problem long before we know precisely what it is. When I have a *sense* of doubt, I feel the anxiety in my body. It comes from not knowing what to do next, not unlike approaching an unanticipated fork in the road. This dissonance, or discomfort, is an important and useful signal. It says, "stand still and take stock of the situation."

Consider the times that a spouse has initiated divorce proceedings even as the partner thought that everything in their relationship was fine. Clearly, one spouse was experiencing dissonance (had a problem), while the other was comfortable (didn't have a problem). Perhaps if there had been better communication between the two, the marriage could have been saved. Without communication, the person with the problem will act to resolve the dissonance alone and focus on feeling better. With more effective decision-making skills, the individual might have chosen other options.

2. State the problem or state what it is that you want. The counselor's responsibility at this point is to facilitate the client's movement from statements like "I want to be happy" to statements of what would constitute happiness. The need is for proposed outcomes that are specific enough that they can be observed, measured, and ultimately celebrated.

3. Once you know what you want, it's time to explore all the ways in which you might attain your goal. This is where the process of "brainstorming" is critical. The counselor's responsibility at this point is to dissuade the client from either/or thinking—from judging and/or evaluating alternatives—and encourage the client to reach for alternatives that are outside of her or his usual modus operandi. During this step in the process, the counselor may hear the clients claim that they would *never* do that. The counselor's task is to encourage even the absurd to be considered as an alternative to be evaluated with all other alternatives in the next steps of the process. This can help to expand the client's thought process.

Sometimes it is useful to invite clients to briefly step outside of themselves and think in terms of what someone else might do. This can provide the freedom to express possibilities that might not otherwise have come forth.

It's been my experience that alternatives that are extreme are often not presented by clients except with sarcasm or tossed out with an attitude that suggests trying to shock the counselor. The statements that concern me the most are:

I could run away and never come back.
I could kill them.
I could kill myself.
I could just do nothing.

My concern is that too often these are real options that need desperately to be addressed or they stand the chance of becoming the "aces" up the sleeve of the client. They would be options that would not have had the benefit of careful scrutiny without the counselor's assistance.

What are the potential consequences of each of these options?
What is the potential cost/gain to you (client)?

Personally, I consider discussion of options of this magnitude so critical that I would go so far as to present them if they are not set forth by the client. It frightens me not to have them out in the open. If they are brought up by the client, whether sarcastically, confrontationally, or casually, I would accept them as any other option to be discussed.

4. Now the task begins of considering the potential consequences (negative and positive) of each of the possible alternatives. This is the step in the process that includes value judgments. An alternative that violates an individual's value system could possibly create more distress than the original problem. However, sometimes this is the point at which values must be examined to determine to whom the value belongs. Is it indeed the client's value or is it a value imposed by someone else? Needless to say, we seem to sometimes inherit values that we fail to examine for ourselves unless someone calls them to our attention. This could cause a temporary detour in the decision-making process but it is deserving of attention.

Let's remember that in considering potential consequences, we are speculating and, therefore, the language we use should reflect our speculation, words such as *might, probably, could.* In addition, we are talking about cost to the client. If you want something, then you buy it and pay for it, trade for it, give time to it, or owe for it. Rarely is there something for nothing that is of any value whether it is a commodity, an experience, or a relationship. In this step, the client identifies probable "cost" and probable gain for each alternative. The next task is for the client to select an option.

5. Selecting an option should be based on the perceived likelihood of getting the greatest value for the time and effort that exercising the option will require. This is the client's judgment call, and it is based on the seriousness of the "want," the perceived value of the "cost," value of the "gain," and the individual's commitment to working for it.

Probably most difficult for any of us is to watch another human being self-destruct or hurt another person. Unquestionably, we are bound by our professional, ethical, and moral standards to report such plans to the appropriate authorities. However, individuals can self-destruct in ways that are beyond our control (i.e., alcoholism, gambling, etc.), and sometimes we are unable to facilitate change. The control over choice is not ours, as frustrating as that may be sometimes.

At this point, I consider it important to remind clients that up to now the process has been essentially theoretical. The *real* consequences can be evaluated only after the chosen option has been acted on. One must then keep in mind that other options still exist, and that one might return to the process if necessary. That's the reason we do not ask clients to select the "best" option. We ask that they select what they think *might* be best.

6. Now the plan. Like starting out on a trip without a map, the whole process is apt to fall apart without a plan of action. Someone once said, "If you don't know where you're going, you could end up somewhere else." The plan is a statement of what the client will do and how the client will do it. The commitment is completed with a statement of "when."

A stated time to begin action on the plan is as vital as any other step in this process. It changes from "when the opportunity presents itself" and becomes the need to create the opportunity. Therefore, it is incumbent on the counselor to discuss with the client whatever the client thinks could get in the way of action. This is the time in the process of establishing the client's commitment to the plan that the counselor must be sure that "what ifs" are thoroughly explored. This is an important part of teaching clients how to get ready to follow through with behavioral commitments they have established. Some useful "what ifs" might be

What if she's not home when I call?
What if he storms out of the room when I try talking with him?
What if I get really nervous and can't bring myself to follow my plan?
What if . . . (Add thoughts of your own.)

Now the client is ready to implement the plan.

7. Measuring the effect of the plan can then be done along the way as the client brings back to counseling sessions the successes and the bumps along the way. During this time, the plan may be modified or even discarded if necessary.

8. If the plan works in reality as it seemed to work in theory, there will be an elimination of dissonance and your client will have experienced a process that can be capsulized and carried forward to the problems of life that haven't happened yet.

If the plan does not eliminate or greatly diminish the dissonance, the client may choose an alternate option, or both counselor and client may need to go back to #2 and examine whether the client accurately perceived and stated what was wanted. He may have stated that he wants better communication with his wife when what he really wants is to not be accountable to anyone. That would be a wholly different scenario.

In the most effective counseling I have ever seen, the decision-making process is first modeled by the counselor, and is presented as an integral part of the facilitative process of counseling. The steps of the decision-making procedure are identified as the counselor moves the process along. The following examples show the kinds of statements and questions a counselor might use to encourage a client through the process.

Now that you have clearly stated the problem that seems to be causing your discomfort . . . (state problem)

What are the many options that could possibly make things better for you? . . . (identify options)

What do you think would be the benefit you would get from doing that? . . . (pros of option)

How difficult would it be for you to do that? . . . (cons of option)

What might the consequences of exercising that option be for you? . . . (cons of option)

Which of the options seems most promising to you at this time? . . . (selection)

What exactly is your plan of action? . . .

When will you do it? . . . (action plan)

And then together we can look at how it worked out for you . . . (evaluation)

In summary, the counselor can then assist the client in identifying the steps by using the language of the process (problem, options, consequences, selection, action, commitment, evaluation) repeatedly as any and all of the client's concerns are worked through in counseling. Clients will learn the language and begin to utilize the process on their own. Your counseling "tool" has now become your clients' more effective method of problem solving.

COMMUNICATION SKILLS

There is little doubt in my mind that the world would be in better shape, and relationships would be more successful, if we were all more skillful communicators. It's unlikely that we'll attain this goal, but it is surely worth striving toward.

The desire for more effective communication is openly stated by many clients, or often quickly observed as a need by many counselors. Clients may tell us that they wish they were better understood by friends, teachers, partners, parents, children, and other associates. Many will tell us of feelings they have that they wish they could share with someone significant in their life. Some will tell us that they wish someone significant in their life would share feelings with them. Some clients express demands and make accusations in their relationships and then are surprised when the responses they get are defensive or hostile.

I believe that, first, we must recognize that people have different styles of communicating. Some people tend to think out loud when working toward an answer to a question. Others will verbalize only their response. Neither style is a problem if the two people attempting to communicate have the same style, but it is potentially a big problem if they do not.

Internal Style: Honey, would you like to have dinner out tonight?

External Style: Well, we have left over pot roast from Tuesday, and I bought salad stuff this afternoon, and I think we said we'd work with the kids on their reports and . . .

Internal Style: (interrupting) Just yes or no is all I want.

External Style: Well, if that's the way you feel about it, no thanks!!

The result of this "could be simple" transaction might be that they argue later about their mutual annoyances, or perhaps they'll choose not to speak to each other at all, with an unpleasant dinner at home for each of them. It didn't have to happen that way if they were mindful of their different styles.

Internal Style: Honey, I'm going to watch the news for a while. Let me know in about half an hour if you're up to having dinner out tonight.

(later)

External Style: I thought about it and tomorrow would really be better; then we can keep our promise to the kids tonight.

Internal Style: Great, then tomorrow it is.

A pleasant dinner tonight and a pleasant dinner tomorrow. It can be so simple if we work *with* differences.

When working with two people, it doesn't take very long to discover whether their styles of communicating are compatible or not. You'll hear it and you'll see it if you listen and look. If they are not, it becomes important for you to help them see the difference and help them find the way to work it through so that they may feel accepted with their different styles.

Second to differing styles is the expressed desire of many clients to be better understood and to have their feelings regarded as important. These are often the same people who are least effective in sharing their feelings even as they think they are trying.

Husband: I feel that she's terribly inconsiderate. I've told her a million times to fill the gas tank in our car when it's below a quarter full. I'm working twelve hours a day and I shouldn't have to worry about gas in the car.

Wife: So I forget sometimes. What's the big deal?

Husband: What's the big deal? Then I end up late for work and that's the big deal.

Counselor: How do you feel when that happens?

Husband: I told you: I feel that she's inconsiderate.

Counselor: Always inconsiderate?

Husband: Of course not. She's usually a very considerate person, but not when she doesn't fill the gas tank.

Counselor: And how do you feel when she isn't considerate about that?

Husband: I feel angry.

Counselor: Angry?

Husband: Well, maybe really hurt that she didn't seem to care about how my day gets started.

Counselor: What would you like to say to your husband?

Wife: I guess I never really looked at it that way. I'm really sorry. I do care a lot about how your day gets started, and I know I'll remember that now that I understand.

When a relationship has some basically sound aspects to it, there is very little difficulty in helping it become even more sound if we can illustrate for our clients how important sharing feelings can be and how much anger can be avoided. This husband initially used the word *feel* and then omitted the feeling. He is hardly alone in doing this, and helping to achieve that awareness may often facilitate a new level of understanding between two people. In addition, it can be very helpful to call clients on labels and absolutes. His use of *inconsiderate* without modification could have taken their exchange to a highly volatile level of attacking and defending centering on consideration. That's not to say that might not be the real issue, but it does call for clarification. If his answer had been, "Yes, she's inconsiderate lots of times," that would have taken us from an issue of more effective communication to different, and possibly more threatening, issues in this relationship. This is where the tools of decision making and communication join together to make for highly effective counseling.

Using the illustration of the partner who works twelve hours a day and the Restated Decision-Making Process in the previous section, write out the scenario that might take place with the focus on promoting communication within the family.

What if the working partner feels isolated from the family?
What if the family is angry that this person is rarely available?
What if the working partner feels hurt and unappreciated?
What if the family feels neglected and unloved?
What if the family wants it all?

Last, but not by any means least, is "feedback." Sharing feelings and taking ownership are the essential factors in giving helpful "feedback" (a word too loosely used to describe almost any response). *Helpful* feedback is critical to effective communication, which in turn yields more successful relationships.

To achieve statements of effective feedback, we need first to define our terms.

Ownership = *I* statements *only*

Feelings = What I experience emotionally

Description of behavior = What someone did that prompted my emotional reaction

(Example: I feel hurt when you use that tone of voice and then I stop listening to what you're saying.)

Some would argue that each person is responsible for his or her feelings and can choose not to get hooked. I fully agree with the premise, and, in some cases, the appropriate choice would be to work with the issue of "hurt" as a personal issue. However, I don't see this as an absolute rule, nor do I see it often successful. When the dynamic of the relationship is the issue, it may be equally valuable to promote the sharing of feelings in a constructive way rather than to work to change the feelings.

In the example of a husband–wife exchange I used, there was no accusation put forth that would precipitate an argument, even if the response seemed to call for one.

> **Response:**   You're telling me that I'm supposed to change my tone of voice?
>
> **Initiator:**   No. I'm just telling you that when I feel hurt it's hard for me to hear you.

I contend that acquiring the skill to give helpful feedback can be the factor that can save many relationships and foster greater intimacy through sharing. The problem that I see when I suggest that this is a skill to be taught to clients is that some of us (counselors) may need to practice it for ourselves first.

Communicating effectively can add considerable depth to the relationship between two significantly related individuals. Too often, I find that very little is communicated regarding the positives that exist between people. It appears to me that, in many relationships, the behaviors that "please" are taken for granted and receive little acknowledgment. I have seen this in partnerships, between parents and children, between teacher and students, and between employers and employees. On the contrary, particularly from clients, there appears to be no shortage of complaints and disappointments that are verbalized or accumulated for future "dumping" or rebellion.

Another possible problem is what I refer to as the "mind-reading syndrome," often indicated by an accusatory *if*-clause.

> If you really love me, you would know what I want.
>
> If you really cared about me, you would know that what you said would really hurt me.
>
> I haven't told you about the scars I carry from the past, but I expect that you can guess.

Communication, as I see it, is the key to the highest level of intimacy and caring. Like Tevye in *Fiddler on the Roof,* when he asked his wife if she loved him, she responded, "I wash your sox, I mend your clothes, . . . ," but she failed to answer his question. Instead, she listed the things she did for him.

Not everyone needs to hear the words for which Tevye was asking, but I believe that everyone needs to feel the essence of those words as each defines "essence." The partner who is at work twelve hours a day may be driven by love and the desire to provide well for the family. If the family feels loved by time spent together, for them time, not money, is the "essence" of love. This requires open communication to clarify values and to achieve greater success in the family relationship. Too often, inadequate communication can ruin things for very well-intentioned people. I believe that demonstrating and teaching communication skills can often turn a painful relationship around.

Many clients seek counseling to address the "Big C," their need for a sense of greater control over their lives. We have the means for helping them with this issue when we have succeeded in integrating these counseling tools into our counseling sessions. I have found that control is often the very essence of many, if not most, problems. First and foremost, we assist clients in recognizing that there are many events in life that are beyond their control. The application of the decision-making process can be extremely valuable in achieving this understanding. It will not provide happiness, but it can provide the understanding that often we can only control how we respond to those events that are beyond our control. I consider this to be critical to a sense of reality-based personal empowerment.

Teaching for improved and more effective communication is an additional process that can facilitate empowerment and a greater sense of control. It provides the opportunity for clients to be less hidden with their feelings, their needs, and their desires. The responses that they receive to their openness can provide them with the information that they need to go on to make better choices for themselves and, thereby, gain greater control over the quality of their lives.

SUMMARY ACTIVITY

1. What is your assessment of *your* decision-making skills?
2. How do you approach the process of deciding about issues or situations that are important to you?
3. How will you "teach" more effective decision making to your clients?
4. What's your assessment of your communication skills?
5. Who are the people in your life who know what gives you pleasure and what causes you pain?
6. What are some of your old emotional "sore spots"?
7. How do you handle them with significant people in your life (i.e., partner, parents, children, boss, best friend)?
8. What can you work on to communicate more openly and effectively with others?
9. How will you do it?
10. What control issues have you been able to resolve through the application of your decision-making and communication skills?

CHAPTER 7

QUESTIONABLE
COUNSELING PROCEDURES

There are counseling techniques and, then again, there are counseling techniques. Many of them work effectively and achieve the desired impact. Unfortunately, there are other procedures that may be accompanied by the very best intentions, yet they may fail to produce positive results. Sometimes such procedures can even have an extremely negative effect on the client and the counseling relationship.

LEADING

Leading is the process whereby counselors take clients in a direction where they think the clients will reap the most benefit. Surely this is done with good intentions, but there are potential problems in the use of this procedure. We could be faced with the possible lack of readiness on the part of the client to go this way at this time. Due to perceived differences in priorities between client and counselor, there can be a lack of commitment or resistance on the part of the client to travel on this path. Worst of all, the chosen direction may represent a total miscalculation on the part of the counselor.

I have often heard counselors state that they are obliged to make a choice for the client because the client has presented so much material. I see the counselor's responsibility somewhat differently. I contend that, if the counselor is unable to assist the client in making *issue* connections between various situations that have been presented, it then behooves the counselor to simply *ask* where the client wants to begin. What is most critical for the client? The client is the one most likely to have the answer.

This is simple enough to do if we, as counselors, will resist the temptation to be in charge. Who will make these choices for the client outside of counseling? How will clients learn to take better care of themselves if we present ourselves as caretakers? I have found that clients will take counselors where they need to go when they are ready and in response to facilitative *what* and *how* questions.

GIVING ADVICE

Giving advice ranks right up at the top of my list of counseling taboos. I believe that, if counselors choose to give advice, they must also be committed to sharing the resulting consequences, whether positive or negative.

If your advice to a client results in success, you own a piece (maybe even all) of the success achieved. What a shame to deprive a client of the opportunity to own it all! The client may be grateful to you, but will have achieved little sense of personal pride. There's no question in my mind that advice that works can save lots of time and effort for the client. However, saving time and effort is hardly the way to measure effective counseling. Awareness, discovery, and the development or honing of skills will save the client time, effort, distress, and failure many times over in the long run.

Then, of course, there's the other side of giving advice. Suppose, just suppose, the advice given by the counselor has negative results. Let's take the case of the client who is in an extremely difficult or unsatisfying relationship and your advice is that the first thing she needs to do is leave the relationship. She agrees that is the way to go. On your advice and with your support, she executes the plan you have chosen for her. Down the road, she has financial difficulties. She's now supporting herself at an entry-level job. How willing are you to help her financially? Suppose she's terribly lonely on the weekends. How available will you be to spend social time with her? Suppose that she ultimately concludes that a bad, but steady, relationship is better than being alone and on her own. Who's to blame for where she is now? She did, after all, get advice from a trained professional.

What do we do if the client directly asks for our advice or our opinion? My suggestion is that the client's question should be answered with a question that goes right back to the decision-making process.

> **Client:**   What do *you* think I should do?
>
> **Counselor:**   Based on all the options we've discussed, what do you think might work best for you?
>
> **Client:**   What do *you* think about the choice I'm making?
>
> **Counselor:**   Let's look again at the potential results that you anticipate from that choice, from the best to the worst possibilities.

Go right back to highlight and reexamine the client's chosen option, focusing on how the client is prepared to handle each of the possible consequences.

I caution against giving advice. It is not what counseling is about, and it will not effectively replace facilitating the acquisition of decision-making skills. Let's leave "advising" to medical doctors, lawyers, and accountants.

SARCASM

The use of sarcasm is a tricky business. First and foremost, there must be a high level of trust between client and counselor before it can even be considered as a counseling tool. I would have to be very sure that not only do I know my client but that my client knows me. Only then would I even consider playing with words.

> **Client:** I guess I really showed her a thing or two about telling me what to do.
>
> **Counselor:** How do you feel now?
>
> versus
>
> **Client:** I guess I really showed her a thing or two about telling me what to do.
>
> **Counselor:** (sarcastically) You surely showed her!! That'll teach *her* a lesson.

Will the counselor's sarcastic reaction help the process? Maybe. Maybe not. It could serve to help the client hear himself or it could reinforce the client's attitude and choice of behavior. I want to be extremely clear about the client's trust in me, the client's vulnerability in the situation being discussed, and the client's view of our relationship. I want to be better able to predict the outcome before I choose sarcasm as a counseling tool.

SELF-DISCLOSURE

How much of myself do I share with the client? How much does the client want to know about me? How much about me do I want known? How much is absolutely relevant to the client's issue? These are questions I have often heard from counselors. My response comes in the form of a question: . . . Who is the focus of this counseling session? Obviously, the answer is "the client."

The client may want to know a great deal about you and your life. I consider that information to be irrelevant to the client's issues, even if you have experienced similar events. Your divorce is not the client's divorce nor is any other event exactly the same. You each have at least somewhat different factors that pertain to any given event and, as a result of different life experiences, you are likely to have somewhat different reactions. Sharing your story may be interesting but it is not apt to be particularly helpful. In fact, it may even be heard as advice. With this in mind, you might want to give some thought to making statements like "I know what you're feeling. I've been there too," or "Oh, I really know how difficult that is."

I maintain that you do *not* know how difficult it is for this person. You only *know* how difficult it was for you. I think it's fair to say that no two people experience the events of life in *exactly* the same way. Therefore, it might be most useful to keep the focus where it belongs, on the client. You might simply return the ball to the client's court with a question.

> **Counselor:**   How would my being divorced be useful to you?
>
> **Client:**   You'd know what I'm feeling.
>
> **Counselor:**   Only you can know precisely what you're experiencing. Tell me about it.

My view is that self-disclosure by the counselor would best serve the client if it was limited to acknowledging resulting feelings rather than indicating shared events, for example, "I've also been confused when I've been bombarded by a great many choices at once," "I know how new experiences have created anxiety for me on some occasions," or "I have also had a sense of trepidation when making changes or working to adjust to changes that have occurred that impact me."

DESCRIBING TECHNIQUES

Your client has stated that a particular relationship is a problem. Let's say that you think it would be useful to understand the dynamic that takes place when your client interacts with the teacher or supervisor at work, as the case may be. Let's go further and agree that you've determined that to hear what generally transpires might clarify the situation for both you and your client. As a result, the technique you have chosen to use is one of role playing. You have a choice to make. You could describe the procedure by explaining to your clients that you want them to pretend that. . . . and then you want them to respond to what was said as they usually would and so on. Or, you could just do it.

> **Client:**   Sometimes my boss gets really angry with me.
>
> **Counselor:**   What does he say?
>
> **Client:**   He says that I don't . . .
>
> **Counselor:**   (interrupting) Try saying it as if he's saying it to you now.
>
> **Client:**   Jim, I'm really sick and tired of having to be on your case for every job to be done on time.
>
> **Counselor:**   And your response . . . ?

Client: I usually say . . .

Counselor: (interrupting) Try saying it as if you're answering him, Jim.

In only moments the client is likely to understand taking both parts in the situation with his boss. You can then have him focus on his boss's perspective and have him challenge the excuses he offers. All of this can usually be accomplished without any explanation of the technique of role reversal.

Similarly, when working with a client who is nervously preparing for an interview or a presentation before an audience, there is generally no need to explain rehearsing or role-playing. Very simply, you invite the client to present to you and the deed is done.

There are two advantages I see to just *doing it* without setting the stage: First, precious time isn't wasted on teaching a lesson on how it's done; second, you minimize the opportunity for anxiety to build in the client and resistance to develop as a result.

Surely, there can be exceptions to what I'm proposing. One such exception might be the client you are working with who is immediately intimidated by the unknown. This client may not be able to proceed without some prior explanation of what will take place. In any case, don't contaminate a useful technique with too much talk. Be succinct in your description.

FACILITATING AWARENESS

Clients will often tell us that their relationship is in trouble. What is the problem? Clients may tell us that very little in their lives gives them a sense of satisfaction. What is the problem? Clients may say that they have no luck, and nothing ever seems to go their way, or that they can't seem to get anything right. What is the problem? These are examples of statements of "being" without the identification of *the problem*. This leads to the need for counseling to facilitate awareness of what the specific problem(s) may be, the client's role in the problematic situation, a better situation for which to strive, and the *power* to create change.

Without awareness of a problem, there is no reason to change behavior. Without awareness of a goal, there is no motivation to strive toward something new. Without awareness of our capacity to change, there is no confidence in our ability to change ourselves or our circumstances. With awareness, a new way of regarding ourselves and our circumstances can open up for us. However, if the process of our psychological development ceases at the stage of awareness, we have attained little more than added discomfort, frustration, and disappointment in our lives.

I have often heard counselors and, for that matter, clients as well talk about the joy of awareness. On the contrary, I consider awareness to be an excruciating burden *if* it is accepted as an end in itself. In my opinion, awareness should serve as the open door to a plan of action that is then implemented. I believe that it would be healthier to leave the door shut if planned action does not ensue. In a counseling relationship, it is the counselor's responsibility to focus on the *whole* process or not to focus at all.

There is also another type of situation in which awareness without action can be seriously deficient. To illustrate my point, I'll share with you a sad but true story.

I was working with a couple with some serious problems in how they communicated with each other and the ways in which their relationship was in trouble. They each had expectations for how they wanted to be treated by the other. One was open to behavioral change in order to live a more positive and fulfilling life together. The other was stuck with awareness. This person had been in counseling for a long period of time and took away from it the understanding of how dysfunctional his family had been and continues to be. He had uncovered every harsh and painful truth regarding his upbringing and that was that. What he brought to his new family (wife) was all the unresolved pain of his upbringing and an explanation for what prevents him from changing his demands and his controls. He came from a very dysfunctional family and he holds them responsible for how he behaves today. What it comes down to for him is, "That's the way they were, that's the way I am, and that's the way I'll always be." (They did it and I am simply a victim of circumstances beyond my control.)

I probably don't have to tell you that, as a result, he did everything he could to control everything and everyone in his adult life and no amount of control would ease his pain. It saddened me to see where his experience in counseling had left him. He was very much aware of the basis for his problems, but was not counseled toward an action plan to rid himself of the "demons" and gain control over how he lives his life.

Did he terminate his counseling too soon? Was his victim role challenged by his counselor? Did he have the opportunity in counseling to explore alternatives to the victim role? I can't be sure of the answers to these questions, but I am very certain that little good will come of the awareness he took from his experience as a client. In order to act, one needs to have a plan of action. In order to formulate such a plan, one must be aware of what needs to be changed. Imagine for yourself the burden of awareness if you realized that your relationship with a family member, friend, or colleague could become more positive if you were to change your behavior. Imagine not following through with an action plan. Now, who's to blame? Who did you blame before you realized your power? How comfortable with your anger are you now?

I can't imagine a more questionable counseling tool than the facilitation of awareness if it is regarded as an end in itself. Awareness is the beginning of a process, not the end!

CELEBRATING CLIENTS

Clients who are working hard and accomplishing a great deal will have much to celebrate. Often they will look to you for confirmation of their success. If you provide that confirmation, I believe you are unwittingly helping the client take a step backwards. Keep in mind that, despite your best facilitation and the absence of advice-giving, you will always be perceived by clients as the "authority," the parent, the teacher, the potential approver. Consider the difference for a client's continued growth based on the counselor's responses in these two scenarios.

Client: I really understand that now.

Counselor: Good for you.

versus

Client: I really understand that now.

Counselor: You sound pleased. Now what can that understanding do for you?

Client: I really kept my promise to you that I would call my father this week and invite him for dinner.

Counselor: Wow! You really did it this time. I'm really pleased.

versus

Client: I really kept my promise to you that I would call my father this week and invite him for dinner.

Counselor: You sound satisfied that you followed through for yourself. Now what?

Praise can be a significant block toward effective counseling. It can be as damaging to the process as it would be if we were critical. Our role is not to be judgmental. Therefore, neither praise nor criticism are appropriate. To provide either would continue our clients' dependency on external forces, which does not help to develop independence and personal growth.

You and I are in the process of counseling to facilitate self-awareness, effective decision making, communication skills, and to promote behavioral change and independence. The most significant way in which we can celebrate our client's success is by turning each request for praise back to the client for self-approval and the joy that comes with having achieved meaningful accomplishments. If we begin with praise from us, we must move to self-praise as we further the process of growth. The celebration is in the pleasure the client experiences, not in our words of congratulations.

There is one major exception to the position I've stated. If we are working with clients who are extremely limited in their ability to gain insight into their behavior, our approach would necessarily be different from the beginning toward any end that might be achieved. Our style of counseling would appropriately be more directive and more concrete than what I have presented. These clients are likely to benefit most from highly structured behavior-modification techniques. This calls for the most basic parenting skills, involving cause and effect. However, unlike more usual parenting, a weaning process from external control may never be fully attained.

When determining the choices that you make as you work to enhance the counseling process, you will need to apply the very same decision-making process that you will try to facilitate with your clients. Selecting counseling tools that work is a process that calls for awareness of your client's limitations, if any exist, knowledge of your options, choices that reflect your values, a clear picture of your goals, reality testing that comes with practice, and a critical examination of results.

SUMMARY ACTIVITY

As you go through your counseling sessions, listen to yourself and ask the following questions.

- How is the agenda for the counseling session established?
- How often have you given advice or advice in disguise?
- What could you have done instead?
- What is your reaction to the use of sarcasm in counseling?
- What do you say when the client asks about your experiences?
- How do you keep the focus on the client when the client asks for your opinion?
- How do you incorporate a specific activity into a counseling session?
- What do you think about the value of facilitating awareness?
- What do you do when you feel satisfied by what your client has achieved or when you are disappointed?

CHAPTER 8

GRAMMATICALLY CORRECT VERSUS EFFECTIVE COUNSELING

Words, words, and more words! Listening to words, deciphering meanings behind the words we hear, and responding to the words we hear and the words that are unspoken—that's what counselors do.

> *Language n.* 1. words and their use. 2. a system of words used in one or more countries. 3. a system of signs or symbols used for conveying information . . . (Adapted from the *Oxford American Dictionary* (OAD) 1980).*

Language is surely the primary vehicle for our profession. Sometimes clients add to their verbal statements with body language that may offer clues as to the veracity of their words, but even then it's the spoken word that clarifies meaning for both the client and the counselor.

Let's look first at how many, if not most, of us have come to use language in our day-to-day interactions with others. How do you react to these statements?

I must get this done today.
I'm sorry but I cannot pick you up at the airport on Tuesday.
I really need to find green shoes for this outfit.
I feel that her behavior is inappropriate.
I can never get anything right.
She always criticizes my decisions.

In all likelihood we would agree that there are no grammatical errors in any of these statements. Now let's examine them more closely. Let's look into the words and, perhaps, even beyond the words themselves and into their potential meanings and the possible ways of reacting to them.

---

*All subsequent definitions in this chapter are adapted from this dictionary.

IMPERATIVES

must auxiliary verb. used to express necessity or obligation, certainty, insistence

I must get this done today. My reading of this statement suggests to me that the necessity of what *must* get done is so imperative that, if it were not to get done, there would be extremely dire consequences. Surely that is a possibility. However, I suggest to you that may not be the case nearly as often as the statement is made by you, by me, and by clients.

More often than not, however, *must* indicates any one of various intentions and concerns for consequences.

- I'd prefer to get this done today and, thereby, be done with it.
- I want to get it done today and, thereby, not have to accept the consequences of not having gotten it done.
- Perhaps if I do this today, I can use it as an excuse for not doing something that I'm trying to get out of doing.
- My pattern of behavior is to set up tasks that are not likely to be completed in the time frame I've established and, thereby, I set myself up to fail.

To be more honest and even kinder to myself, I could say what I really mean, which might be,

I would like to get this done today . . .
- and be finished with it.
- and not lose a grade for being late.
- rather than go to the movies with you. This is really important to me.
- and feel good about my accomplishment.

cannot opposite of *can*; expresses ability or knowledge of how to do something

I'm sorry but I cannot pick you up at the airport on Tuesday. This statement would be accurate if any of the following are true:

I do not have an operating vehicle.
I am physically unable to drive.
I will be out of town.
I am truly sorry (as opposed to being relieved).

What are the real circumstances? What could I say that would be truthful without being unkind? What could I say that would be in my best interest without being unfeeling? What could I say so that I won't end up being annoyed with the person who asked and even more annoyed with myself for having agreed to do what I did not want to do?

THAT'S WHO I AM

There is one statement that I've heard repeatedly in counseling sessions from clients: "I can't help it!" What I hear is, "That's the way I've always been," "That's just who I am," or "That's my personality." To begin with, I believe that your personality and my personality can best be described as the collection of behavioral responses we have learned over the years that we consistently continue to employ. As a result of this belief, it is my contention that you and I can learn new behavioral responses to situations, even as "old habits die hard." Therefore, I suggest to you that "I can't help it" means "I won't help it," unless we're dealing with a given physical limitation. Are there also psychological limitations? Sure there are, but isn't that what counseling can be about? Change is scary. Support for change is often critical for success. Motivation to change is vital. Preparedness to deal with the effects of change is essential. Effective counseling can facilitate the process.

NEEDS AND WANTS

need verb. to require, to be a necessity

I really need *to find green shoes for this outfit.* Obviously, I've taken this to the absurd (even as I've said this myself), just to make my point. Let's face it, green shoes would only be a necessity for someone whose occupation required them as part of a uniform for work. Even then, the individual could choose to seek another job. Do I *want* green shoes to match my outfit? Indeed I do. Do I *need* green shoes? Only if I refuse to consider an alternative or if I insist on creating a crisis situation for myself.

What about the client who says, "I need to call my mother every day"? Maybe this statement is true; maybe it's not. Maybe this individual calls his or her mother everyday because she'd be angry otherwise. Perhaps this person would "feel" guilty if the call were not made. Guilty of what?

What about the parent who says, "I need your room cleaned before you can go out"? Is this an accurate statement? Could it be that the way you keep your room is an embarrassment to the parent? Could it be that the relationship is built on confrontation, and it's the only way he or she knows to maintain contact with you? Could it be that this parent has a desire to control each and every aspect of your environment? What could it be that the parent is really dealing with? Is it the room? Is it the relationship? Is it you? Or do I mean *want* when I say *need*? Perhaps I'm wishing that we might share the same values; that our relationship was based on caring and understanding, rather than arguments and battles; that I could be less rigid in the expectations and demands I place on others; or that I wouldn't feel rejected when you don't do what I *need* done. The possibilities certainly sound like grist for the counseling mill to me. What do you think?

feel verb. to be conscious of, to be aware of being. 2. to be affected by. 3. to have a vague conviction or impression of something. 4. to have an opinion

I feel that her behavior is inappropriate. This statement uses *feel* in sense three or four. It certainly does *not* mean "to be conscious of" or "to be affected by" in this example. In order to be more precise, I would rewrite it: "In my opinion, her behavior is inappropriate."

As you read my revision, you might want to question it. I'll explain. I have come to cringe at the use of *feel* to mean "think" as I read and hear it used thoughtlessly by professional counselors, teachers, parents, politicians, and, of course, clients. I cringe, not because of any grammatically incorrect usage, but because we seem to use the word *feel* to suggest that we are regularly making our feelings known to others, even as we may rarely (if ever) tell others how what they are saying or doing affects us. And I have heard clients repeatedly express their pain over the extent to which they consider their feelings to be disregarded when they are certain that they consistently have shared them. Have they really?

Let me restate the example in a way that could be more informative: "I am hurt by her lack of attention." Yes, I may really *think* her behavior is inappropriate. Yes, I may *think* that I deserve better from her. Yes, I don't like the way in which she is treating me. But . . . how do I feel??? Have I told her how her behavior affects me? Will all people see her behavior as inappropriate? Will *all* people feel hurt by the behavior? Probably not. Therefore, if I'm talking about how I *feel,* perhaps I ought to consider saying what I'm feeling.

Probably one of the most important reasons for making this distinction in relationships is to foster knowing one another in a way that can bring people closer together, and to provide the information to one another that can ultimately *avoid* hurt and anger. I believe that we often foster the probability of being hurt through our unwillingness to share our feelings with others. To share our feelings is certainly to make ourselves vulnerable to deliberate acts that can be painful. However, perhaps somewhat naively, I don't think that most people are out to hurt us. If some people are deliberate in causing us pain, I consider that to be very important information to have. That's not where I would want to be. With the knowledge of their intent, I can be motivated to move on to safer and more caring relationships.

How do we relate the distinction between what we think and what we feel to counseling? How can we possibly avoid the distinction if we, as counselors, are to employ any of the counseling techniques set forth by our theorists? For example, how can we base our counseling on Carl Rogers without consideration for "congruence," which he has described as the harmony of what we are feeling, what we are thinking, and how we are behaving (Rogers, 1980)? How can we employ the basics of Gestalt Therapy (Perls, Hefferline, & Goodman, 1951) without attention to the feelings that are communicated through actions rather than through words? How can we help clients to reframe (LaClave & Brack, 1987) their thinking if we do not attend to the distinction between feelings and thoughts?

How can we refer to the counseling techniques of Albert Ellis without reference to the A + B = C paradigm (Ellis & Harper, 1975). To utilize the most basic concepts set forth by Ellis, we would certainly have to facilitate the identification of a precipitating event (A), the thoughts generated as a response to the event (B), and the resulting feelings (C). How can we challenge irrational thoughts in anticipation of changing behaviors if we do not first help our clients recognize that they may be unable to support some of their thoughts with "facts"? How can we even initiate this process without distinguishing between feelings and thoughts?

Individually, we think different thoughts in response to the same stimulus. We think them in different languages as a condition of what our culture has taught us and as a result of our experiences. Different from thoughts, feelings are more limited in diversity. Cold is cold and hot is hot and the statement, "I feel cold" or "I feel hot," varies only based on an individual's tolerance for the temperature. Neither of these statements is open to debate because it is a statement of how one individual feels physically in reaction to the temperature in the room. The statement, "I think it's too cold in here," is different. The response could be, "I don't think so." Haven't you ever disagreed with someone over whether the window should be open or shut or the heat higher or lower?

Thoughts are debatable, feelings are not! Feelings are physiological and vary depending on each person's unique thought process. Probably the most annoying, and least useful statements, I have ever heard from one person to another is "You really shouldn't feel that way." This can be understood to mean, "I don't feel that way," "I wouldn't feel that way," or "How you feel is your problem." However one understands it, we cannot control how other people feel.

How, then, can we describe our feelings when that is what we want to do? Consider these four statements:

1. I feel that you should be more attentive.
2. I feel as if you're ignoring me.
3. I feel annoyed when you read the newspapers when I'm telling you about my day.
4. It annoys me when you read the newspaper when I'm telling you about my day.

"I feel that" announces a thought, wish, or desire and does not state a feeling. It is usually followed by a directive to someone about how you want them to behave differently. "I feel as if" announces a judgment, and judgments are not feelings. They come from your head. The use of *feel* is an attempt to disguise your judgment so that it cannot be questioned. The statements in three and *four* are both descriptions of a feeling, annoyance, with and without *feel* used explicitly. The statement of a feeling generally does not require the use of the word *feel*, e.g., "I'm cold," "I'm angry," "I'm nervous," "I'm bored," "I'm happy," "I'm sad," and so forth. Now, what are *you* thinking? What are *you* feeling?

GUILT

I believe that we *must* regard language very carefully, very critically, and very consistently in counseling. Let's look at the implications of language usage on the issue of guilt. What is this guilty "feeling" we hear about so often? Over the years, I have asked clients who have referred to *feelings of guilt* to point to the place in their body where they feel this feeling. Time and time again they point to their head. Other than a headache, an earache, or a toothache, it is beyond my ability to identify a *feeling* in my head. I believe that we have created a phrase that is misleading, at best, and not at all useful in a counseling setting. The experience of distress that we often refer to as "feeling guilty" is the reaction we have to the "could'ves," "should'ves," "would'ves," and the reverse of these that we are thinking.

What do you experience within yourself when you have judged yourself as guilty? I have felt embarrassment, shame, discomfort, and so on, and these feelings have registered somewhere in my body other than in my head. So, what causes most people to point to their heads when they describe guilt? The explanation that satisfies me is that, once again, there is the tendency to confuse feelings with thoughts. For example, let's suppose I told my in-laws that I could not attend the dinner party they were having at their home and, as my excuse, I said I had theater tickets for that evening. I might have "felt guilty" for having lied to them and, for "fear" that they would find out that I had lied, not only did I not answer my phone the night of the party, I also called the next day to say how sorry I was to not have been there and told them about the show I had (not really) seen. When speaking to them I felt uncomfortable and embarrassed. Did I "feel guilty"? Technically, no. In my head I was disapproving of my behavior and, as a result, I was physically uncomfortable. In my head, I had judged my behavior as "wrong" and judged myself guilty.

Issues of guilt arise so often in counseling that counselors need a tool for working with them effectively. In my opinion, these are situations in which teaching clients to distinguish between feelings and thoughts can be extremely useful. If we don't want to "feel guilty," we must either change the judgments we make of our behaviors or we must change the way in which we behave. Only then will we not feel the stressful feelings that are the result of the "guilty" verdict that we pronounce on ourselves.

What's wrong with guilt? Most of the time, nothing. In fact, it deters us from running red lights, shoplifting, lying, and other things we might otherwise do. Remember the time the amber light had turned to red and you kept going anyway? Remember that you probably looked in your rearview mirror expecting to see the police. Remember also that your body registered a feeling of discomfort. Potential guilt comes from what we've been taught and what we have come to value. Potential guilt is what makes laws work and creates a basically civilized and acceptable society. Guilt is not a *bad* thing, but it can be inappropriate. When it is inappropriate, we have an important counseling issue, and we must address the thought process or the behaviors in order to eliminate or minimize what can be debilitating feelings.

The most potentially destructive guilt is generally related to actions or the lack of action in the past. This can sometimes be addressed by offering explanations in the present to the offended parties or by reframing one's thinking to allow for forgiveness of one's self. Whatever the process, it is unlikely that anyone can change the feelings without addressing the thoughts or behaviors associated with those feelings.

As a result of my analysis of what guilt is about, I propose that, when a client speaks of "feeling guilty," the most useful questions a counselor can ask are: "Where do you feel it?" "What other name can you give it?" and "What are you thinking (saying to yourself) when you feel it?"

ABSOLUTES

Oh my, the danger of absolutes! The total put-down of self and the all-inclusive accusation.

> I can never get anything right.
> You always criticize my decisions

In the first statement, I hear either the crying out from a negative sense of self that often is the result of the consistent bombardment by significant others in their indiscriminate use of absolutes or the result of unrealistic or misinformed decision making. This sense of failure is then reinforced repeatedly by the individual's self-bashing and poor choices. How do we break the cycle? We challenge the absolutes and we teach decision-making skills.

What I hear in the second statement is a complaint about the behavior of another. How do we change someone else's behavior? The only way I've ever succeeded is by changing the way in which I respond to their behavior.

Doing that can send their conditioned expectations reeling and put me in control of my thoughts and feelings.

How do I help the client learn to do this? With great difficulty, because so many people I know want desperately to change others. If only I knew how to magically accomplish this, I'd give up counseling and become a wizard. Until that time, I will continue to work with my clients to help them to reframe their thinking, to rely less on the opinions of others, and to assess their worth using the yardstick of their own values and realistic goals.

PRONOUNS

I would be remiss if I were to conclude my thesis on language without addressing the critical issue of pronouns. I will be brief.

1. Ownership requires "I" statements.
2. "You" statements can often promote an argument.
3. "People" statements refer to everyone and no one simultaneously.
4. "We" statements without prior agreement are subject to challenge.

APPLICATION TO MORE EFFECTIVE COUNSELING

Clarifying language and challenging the specific ways in which clients use language can be a powerful counseling tool. I suggest to you that, before you and I can effectively use this tool, we must each listen carefully to ourselves and determine how well *we* are doing. I'll wager that you'll be as surprised as I was to hear how grammatically correct I could be without saying what I really *needed* to say to communicate more effectively.

We have little reason to believe that clients have addressed the issues that can be generated by their unexamined choice of words. We are constantly bombarded by the use of *musts*, excuses, self-proclaimed guilt, absolutes, and the wanton interchange of needs/wants and feelings/thoughts. Listen carefully to television, radio, parents, teachers, and others, and you may be surprised by how commonplace this situation is in our daily environment. Perhaps it isn't always a problem but, when there is a problem, it may be a critical factor.

As with all that we do in counseling, language use, too, must be addressed with sensitivity so that our engagement with our client is neither disrespectful, demeaning, nor confusing. There are, for example, ways of drawing a client's attention to his or her use of language that I think are counterproductive.

You said *must* but you *really* mean *prefer.* Right?

You said that's your "personality," but you could change if you *really* tried.

You said *need* but I think you *really* mean *want.*

You said *feel* but you *really* mean *think.*

You said "feel guilty" but that's not *really* a feeling.

You said you "have to," but *really* no one has to do anything.

To respond in these ways would be to admonish your client for having less awareness than you do of the subtleties of language. Our aim might rather be to foster understanding of the potentially positive consequences of greater clarity as a result of more accurate language choices. My next list provides alternative ways of getting clients to listen to what they are saying by asking questions rather than making statements.

You said you "must" get that done. What might happen if you didn't?

You said that's your "personality." I'm not sure I know what you mean.

You said you "need." What might happen if you didn't get it? How would you handle that?

You said you "feel" crowded by your parents. What are you thinking when they act that way?

You said you "feel guilty" when you _____. What are you saying to yourself when you do that?

You said you "have to _____." What do you see happening if you don't?

My objective in asking such questions is to confront the language inaccuracies in order to prompt in-depth consideration of the problems that clients may be causing themselves. My long-range goals are also to promote more accurate and open communication, to lessen self-imposed stress, and to facilitate greater honesty in relationships.

SUMMARY ACTIVITY

1. Think of some other examples and examine the words as I've done in this chapter.
   a. What implications do you see for more effective communication?
   b. What implications do you see for more effective counseling?
   c. What implications do you see for some of your relationships with others?

2. Listen to yourself in conversation with others outside of the counseling setting.
   a. Do you say *need* when you mean *want*?
   b. Do you say *feel* when you mean *think*?
   c. Do you say *can't* when you mean *won't*?
   d. What's your arguing style? Do you use labels?
   e. Do you take ownership for your feelings?
   f. Do you give orders?
   g. Do you speak in absolutes (e.g., *must, never, always*)?
3. How can you take advantage of everyday personal interactions to assist you in fine-tuning your use of language?

CHAPTER 9

TERMINATING THE COUNSELING RELATIONSHIP

Little seems to have changed regarding the "when" and "how" of termination in all my years in the counseling profession. We're likely to hear as many opinions as there are counselors debating these issues. Because you have apparently gotten this far in this book, and you have consistently read about my beliefs and my contentions, I will continue to share the same with you regarding terminating the counseling relationship.

THE MORAL AND ETHICAL ASPECTS

As counselors, we have no fewer personal needs, wants, and frailties than many other people. As with most other humans, we are aware of some and unaware of others. This belief on my part leads me to conclude that we are as vulnerable as anyone to temptations that may confront us. I am particularly concerned that, in our profession, we are either paid by the number of clients that we see or we are in some fashion rewarded for keeping our numbers up.

Do I mean to imply that counselors in private practice will deliberately hold onto clients who should be terminated? Perhaps. Do I suggest that agencies sometimes frown on terminating some clients due to the agency's need to maintain the volume that drives funding resources? Perhaps.

The underlying moral and ethical issue that must be faced is the question of whose interest is being served by continuing the counseling relationship. If the answer is anything but *the client*, it would be deceitful, manipulative, unethical, immoral, and unprofessional of us to continue the counseling relationship. There are various circumstances under which the counseling relationship warrants termination.

The first and perhaps the most obvious would be if we are not suitably trained to work with a client's particular circumstances. As I've said, this could be a client who requires a more clinical orientation to counseling than that for which we may have been trained, or someone whose needs may include medication, which would require that we work with a psychiatrist or make appropriate referrals.

The next question is whether or not we are *emotionally* prepared to work with the circumstances brought to us by the client. Is the client dealing with issues of loss? Have we recently experienced a significant loss in our life? Are we prepared to be separate enough from the client's issue in order to counsel effectively, or are we so vulnerable that we are apt to commiserate rather than counsel? When our own vulnerability renders us emotionally unprepared to counsel effectively, we are morally and ethically bound to refer this client to another counselor.

There are also clients who may come to us with issues that are emotional "hot spots" for us. I consider these to be long-standing issues that we cannot or will not handle professionally. For me, that would be an individual who, for *whatever reasons,* has demonstrated severe physical abuse toward children.

I was not an abused child. I have had no significant relationship with anyone who suffered physical abuse as a child. I *have* studied and read much about the circumstances that often promote abusive behavior toward children. I intellectually understand and accept the psychological and environmental circumstances that contribute to and cause someone to physically abuse children. Given all of this, I am unable (actually, unwilling) to have compassion, empathy, caring, or any other counseling attitude requisite for the perpetrator. What makes the situation even worse is that I feel content with my loathing and have consciously chosen not to do anything to change my emotional response. Needless to say, it would be absolutely inappropriate for me to work with a child-abusing client. It would be equally inappropriate for me to share my distaste for such a person.

In no way am I advocating intolerance toward any individual. On the contrary, I am advocating that, if intolerance exists, it is essential that it be recognized, owned, and dealt with appropriately. It is morally and ethically necessary to terminate such a contaminated relationship rather than proceed in a biased manner.

Therefore, my ethical and moral responsibility, as I see it, must be to inform such potential clients that I am not equipped to deal with their situation and to then terminate with an appropriate referral. What about you? What are your biases? What are your unresolved issues? What will you choose to work out in your own therapy as a client? What will you choose to hold onto? How will your answers dictate whom you will counsel?

LACK OF PROGRESS

Another significant reason for termination is a perceived lack of progress. Generally, clients who experience little headway will terminate of their own accord. Sometimes this will be done without any discussion. It might be a canceled appointment with no action to reschedule. It might be a statement of uncertainty as to when they can see you again and assurance that they will call to set a future appointment, which, of course, they do not do. They might choose to say that they are experiencing counseling as a waste of time. I believe that in this case several questions may be appropriate for discussion prior to termination. For example:

Counselor: What are you ready to work on that we have not yet addressed?

or

Counselor: What would you want me to ask you that I haven't asked?

or

Counselor: What are we working to accomplish that might be frightening for you?

Despite all your best efforts, the client may not be ready or willing to proceed. In that case, the best you can do is to assure the client that your door is open in the future. So be it!

On the other hand, you may be the only one who is discontent with what you perceive as lack of progress. For me, this is when I sense almost total resistance to work or the development of client dependency on the relationship. It is at that point that I will actively initiate ending the counseling relationship by confronting the resistance or the dependency. Sometimes, telling the client that I don't see us making progress and suggesting that the client might seek help from someone else, or that perhaps this just isn't the right time, can be just the confrontation with reality that moves the process. Sometimes this happens and sometimes it doesn't. Sometimes, in my own head, I imagine the client telling others that I just "wasn't any good." You know by now that I wouldn't like that one bit, but perhaps in that case I wasn't or perhaps I really was!

Whatever the facts may be, I consider it appropriate to terminate the relationship whether the lack of progress is due to my inability to find a way through the client's resistance or the lack of readiness on the part of the client. In either case, it would be exploitative to just pass time with this person. Let me assure you that this isn't a happy scenario for me. I'd rather be successful in all my counseling endeavors but, as with all efforts, it's very unlikely that this will happen. Am I equally effective with every client? No! Does every client with whom I come in contact like me? No! Do I wish it were different? Of course I do; I'm only human.

You might be asking yourself, what if the client just doesn't like me? In most cases these people will call to cancel their next appointment, stating that they will call again when they know they can make it. Guess what? Of course, they never call again!

PRESET ALLOWABLE COUNSELING SESSIONS

If the number of sessions you may have with a given client is preset by an HMO, your school, agency, or the organization for which you work, I consider it to be critically important to the counseling process that this be discussed with your client at the start. I also consider it vital that the number of remaining sessions be pointed out regularly. I say this because I believe that there are times when urgency can be a strong motivating factor for some clients to get work done.

I don't mean to suggest to you that I support the idea of an external factor determining how many sessions is the right number of sessions for a given client, I don't! Personally, I see it as an affront to our professionalism as counselors. However, as we try to teach our clients, we, too, have realities and "givens" that may not please us, but with which we must work. Therefore, if it's real, use it to advantage!

TERMINATING A SUCCESSFUL EXPERIENCE

Let me begin by saying that I do not believe that I should take responsibility for ending the relationship in most cases. My justification for this position is the same as other opinions I've stated in this text: I am unwilling to accept the notion that I know what is best for the client. This determination should result from a joint evaluation between client and counselor of the changes that have taken place.

For example, a sense of dissonance brought into counseling may have been replaced by a state of well-being because the client can now make decisions and solve problems that are likely to be in the client's best interests. A sense of helplessness or powerlessness may have been replaced by a sense of confidence in the ability to maintain reasonable control over how one lives one's life. The desire for someone else to *fix things* may have been replaced by the confidence that comes with having acquired the skills to fix things on one's own. Success in counseling should not be measured by having found the solution to a particular problem, but rather on the extent to which thought processes, feelings, and behaviors have changed, and skills have been learned.

In my experience, there often appears to be a different perception of when to terminate counseling that seems to sometimes divide along gender lines. Men often seem ready to get up and go when they have intellectually resolved a particular problem. Sometimes this can be almost humorous, as when some men talk about how much they have learned about the importance of sharing their feelings, although they may have not yet demonstrated this behavior toward anyone. The cognition alone will ultimately only create discomfort, and I consider the counseling task as incomplete.

Women, on the other hand, sometimes see themselves ready to terminate counseling when they feel less anxious or feel less stressed, even as they may not yet be able to articulate what they have done behaviorally or cognitively that might be replicated in the future to minimize future stress and anxiety. Again, I consider the counseling task to be incomplete and not ready for termination.

In such cases, I ask my client to respond to questions that summarize the counseling experience, for example:

> How do you see yourself as different from when you first came into counseling?
>
> What new behaviors have you learned that work well for you?
>
> What have you learned to do when you find yourself pulled by old behaviors and/or thoughts that didn't work well for you in the past?
>
> What new skills have you acquired that are helpful to you?
>
> Tell me what you did recently that are examples of how you've used what you've learned.

Internalized Changes = Successful Counseling = Time to Terminate

"COLD TURKEY" VERSUS A WEANING PROCESS

On some occasions clients will come to a counseling session with termination of the counseling relationship already decided. This process of "cold turkey" is my least favorite way to see clients go on their way. My viewpoint is once again based on years of experience and the idea that most of us achieve success when we have recognizable support for the changes we make. I certainly do not want my clients to meet with failure after all the hard work they have done. Therefore, if clients make the statement that they are terminating, I will suggest weaning away. If that is not accepted, I will give them every assurance that I will be available to them if they should decide that they could use the support. This can be a very tricky business because I want to choose my words and present my attitude carefully so as to *not*, in any way, suggest that I don't think they are ready to go on their own. To do so could be a serious blow to whatever sense of self-confidence they have developed.

Essentially, I see my role during termination to be as much a facilitator of the process as with any other stage in the counseling process. To me, that means that I am responsible for assessing where I think we are and then I am responsible for asking important questions. For example, I might take note of the fact that the opening "small talk" is extending well beyond the first minute of the session, and the client is engaging in what I consider to be "visiting" rather than working. In this case I would ask: "__(name)__, what are we working on now?" The client's answer will determine what we do next. In my experience, the client will introduce new material, reopen old material that I may have thought was resolved, but, in fact, was not, or the client may not have anything to offer. Rather than conclude that our work is done, I will ask the client what he or she wants to do. The dialogue may go something like this:

Client: I really don't know. I feel good about what I've learned and changes I've begun to make. Maybe I don't need to come to see you anymore.

Counselor: Maybe not.

Client: What do you think?

Counselor: As with everything else, we've worked on, I think the decision is yours.

Client: It's just been so helpful knowing that I'd see you every week, and it's a little scary to stop.

Counselor: What might make it less scary for you?

Client: What if we tried every other week?

Counselor: We could meet once in two weeks or three weeks or once a month. Whatever you decide.

Client: You really think three or four weeks would be OK?

Counselor (smiling but refusing to budge):   I think the decision has to be up to you. (Noting the client's trepidation) Suppose you decide on once in three weeks, what's the worst that could happen?

Client: I could really want to see you sooner than that . . .

Counselor: . . . and . . . ?

Client: . . . and I'd call to make an appointment sooner. That sounds OK.

Counselor: So we'll set our appointment for three weeks from today, and, during that time, what will you do?

Client: I'll be using everything I've learned here and I'll know that you're here, if I need you.

Counselor: See you then.

Did I have a plan in mind when the client and I entered into this exchange? I certainly did:

■ The client determines termination with my facilitation.
■ The client determines if the process of termination is "cold turkey" or a weaning process.
■ If the client suggests a weaning process, I offer duration options based on my confidence in the client's readiness to succeed. This may have meant the reverse of what was presented in my example. The client

might have initially suggested meeting with me once a month, to which I might have responded that it could be once a month, once in three weeks, or every other week.

- I will *not* make the decision for the client. I'd like to believe that I didn't make decisions for the client throughout our relationship and, therefore, I will not begin at this time. The issues involved are independence and personal responsibility.

- I will respond in a supportive way to the client's nervousness and, thereby, provide an "open door."

- My long-term objective is to encourage stretching the time period until the client and I conclude that perhaps all that's needed is the knowledge of an "open door."

Relevant to this process of termination, I'd like to share what have come to be highlight moments for me in my counseling. I'm referring now to clients whom I had been seeing on a weekly basis who then chose longer periods between sessions, with the understanding that they could call for an earlier appointment if they thought it was needed. For example,

> **Client:**   It feels a little strange not having been here for three weeks. Things got a little out of hand last week and I was about to call. Instead, I asked myself, 'What would Arlene ask me?' and then I did it all by myself.
>
> **Counselor (smiling):**   You sound really pleased.
>
> **Client:**   I really am.
>
> **Counselor:**   So, now what?
>
> **Client:**   I guess I'll just call if I think I need to come back.

And there it is! The best tribute to effective counseling is the client's statement that says, I have the skills. I have the confidence. I can do it myself.

I'd like to point out to my readers that, on occasion, I'll receive a call from former clients whom I may not have seen for a year, or even years. These clients call for what we've labeled a "pep-rally appointment." There are also those clients who make an appointment to share how they have successfully turned things around for themselves, and they want to share their success with "the person who knew them when. . . ."

SAYING "GOOD-BYE"

Counseling, like teaching, has many beginnings and just as many endings. For me, beginnings are somewhat uncomfortable because they are replete with unknowns. Regardless of the great number of classes I have taught over the decades, I continue to experience the anxiety that comes with meeting a new population and presenting a new me who never existed before as I exist on that day. Similarly, I experience this dynamic with each new client.

In saying "good-bye," I have never ceased to experience the emotional aspect of separation from a significant relationship. For me, it is that special combination of the bitter with the sweet. It is the delight shared with my clients who leave more assured, more able, and more competent to deal successfully with their lives. It is also the momentary down feeling, much like I feel when I complete my reading of a book I have truly enjoyed and there just is no more left for me to read. What has worked best for me has been to momentarily stand by the shut door, take a deep breath, smile to myself, and anticipate the next adventure.

SUMMARY QUESTIONS

Here are some questions related to terminating the counseling relationship, with the answers that I consider to be appropriate. Consider my responses, add what you think I've omitted, and delete those with which you disagree. With each addition or deletion, write out your rationale. When this is done, you might meet with some colleagues and debate the elements related to termination. Be prepared for differing viewpoints.

- What is termination?
  It is the end of a generally regular sequence of counseling sessions.

- Is termination always a positive process?
  Hopefully, it is achieved in a caring and responsible manner regardless of the reason for terminating the relationship.

- When is termination appropriate?
  When the counselor is emotionally, or, by training, unsuited to the client's needs; when little or no progress is being achieved over several sessions; when the client and counselor are satisfied that the "job" has been done; or when the client says so.

- What is the "weaning process"?
  It is a systematic increase in time elapsed between counseling sessions to allow for the client's assessment of achievements and the confidence to proceed unassisted.

- What if I don't *like* my client?
  Counseling, unlike friendship, is based on valuing the worth of the individual only. It is not required that client and counselor share interests, viewpoints, experiences, or perspectives on life.

■ What if I have unresolved issues of my own?
In your role as counselor, your sessions are not about you. Your issues belong in sessions where you are the client. Issues that you carry with you disqualify you from working with clients who trigger these issues for you.

■ What is a counseling "pep rally"?
It is an open invitation to terminated clients to contact the counselor at any time for a single session designed to reinforce learning and/or to check out the real-life application of learning by the client. The "pep rally" agenda is established totally by the client.

■ What do I do if a client just stops coming to see me?
Examine what you might have done differently, and then you might consider convincing yourself that the client wasn't ready to work just so you can feel better. Hopefully, this won't happen often. If it does, you might need to take a long hard look at your behaviors, your style, and what you need to learn.

■ How do I know if what I worked to facilitate really made a difference for my clients?
You may sometimes hear from past clients who will tell you, but, most often, you'll never know. Counseling is not a profession that delivers much in the way of applause or awards. I have come to grant myself a bow or two when a new client calls for an appointment based on a referral made by a past client. This suggests to me that I probably did something useful.

CHAPTER 10

"THE MELTING POT" VERSUS "THE MÉLANGE"

My grandparents and my parents arrived on the shore of these United States in the 1920s filled with expectations and dreams of equality. By virtue of the concept of "the melting pot," it might have been expected, by them and by others, that, like the pureed carrot in the vegetable soup, they would add flavor to their new environment even as their identity would become indistinguishable. It didn't happen quite that way.

They continued to look different from many other people in the wide community. They learned to speak a language in public other than their native tongue. They learned the laws, paid their taxes, and became law-abiding citizens of their new country. However, they also retained the religion and rituals that they brought from "the old country," the music that they said was "in their blood," and, most significant of all, they held to the customs and values with which they had been raised.

I believe that this scenario has been repeated in this country since the landing at Plymouth Rock by group after group seeking a better life as well as those who were abducted from their homes and enslaved. If we have succeeded at all in recent years in the integration of diverse cultures into a mainstream society, it has not, in my opinion, been accomplished by minimizing our differences but, rather, by the efforts made to provide equal opportunities and considerations for all. As a result, I do not see a "melting pot" where diversity has disappeared, rather I see a mélange, a mixture, a medley of differences that yields the preservation of cultures and cultural identities and considers differences as a strength within a unified society. However idealistic this may sound, I believe that it is the objective for many of us and the unavoidable reality for others. This multicultural society can be a significant challenge for counselors.

THE CHALLENGE

The challenge for counselors is greater than the diverse groups of people within our society: No two people are exactly alike and, even more important,

97

is the likelihood that no two people have had exactly the same life experience or see the world in exactly the same way. Beyond cultural differences and differences in life experiences, no two people have had exactly the same environment in which to develop, not even identical twins A and B. At the very best, A's twin is B *but* B's twin is A.

Varying environments within our country respond differently to the uniqueness of each of us. Often, this is based on the established norms, expectations, and prejudices of that milieu. In too few environments is the acceptance of diversity the norm. Preconceived judgments and expectations continue to prevail. Our society abounds with people who are in some ways different from us, yet they come to us for counseling. The list of possible differences, combined with the implied differences in values and expectations, is almost endless. There are

    age differences
    gender differences
    ethnic differences
    cultural differences
    socioeconomic differences
    sexual persuasion differences
    educational differences
    religious differences
    political differences
    physical differences, and so on.

All of this is further complicated by the particular perceptions and expectations held by each individual.

Despite all this diversity in the clients that may come to work with us, most counselors cling passionately to the concept of unconditional positive regard strongly emphasized by Carl Rogers: Individuals are valued for the very fact that they exist and that their uniqueness is valued for its own sake and how it enriches all of us.

If this utopian state is to exist anywhere, it must exist in the counseling environment that we share with our clients. The responsibility for this rests with each of us who counsel, and it imposes on us the challenge of careful self-examination and complete honesty. I believe that we must stand still long enough to examine who we are and own the aspects of our prejudices and expectations that fall short of the ideal that I have described. We can surely change what we find that we dislike about our views if we choose to change. After all, that is the underlying contention of the very counseling we are offering to our clients. We can retain any view we choose to retain but then, as with our clients, we have the responsibility to own what we opt to keep and not impose our values on others without being completely open about what we're doing.

In itself, what I've described is a complicated, difficult, and sometimes disturbing task. Yet, it isn't even all that needs to be done. We need to know the specifics of each client's values and expectations that are relevant to the work we will be doing together.

MEETING THE CHALLENGE

There are several elements that I consider to be vitally important in dealing with differences.

1. *We need to do our "homework."* We need to learn about the prevalent mores of people with whom we are working. There are books to read, classes and workshops to attend, and knowledge to be obtained that is crucial for understanding the factors that may influence the decisions and subsequent behaviors that our client may choose.

2. *We need to ask questions.* We need to relate to each client as a unique individual who exists within a variety of normative cultures that may be very different from our own. This creates the need for us to ask questions of our clients so that we can best understand the parameters, the values, and the nonnegotiables with which they function. We need the answer to the question, what should I know about who you are so that I can understand where you are coming from and where you want to be?

3. *We need to respect our uniqueness as well as theirs.* We need to fully recognize and accept that different perceptions and different responses prevail even when different cultural backgrounds are not factors that are involved. There is no other you and there is no other me and so events affect us differently.

Despite the complications caused by differences, there are at least two factors that make it possible for us to meet the challenge of effective counseling: The concept of unconditional positive regard that I referred to earlier, and the fact that there are specific human emotions that we have all experienced. Who has never been frightened? Who has never experienced rejection? Who has never felt hurt? Who has never yearned for acceptance? Love? Caring? These shared aspects enable us to relate to one another affectively even though our experiences may have been significantly different.

BARRIERS TO SUCCESS

The most prevalent barrier that I have seen imposed by counselors has been their well-intentioned effort to facilitate mainstreaming in spite of a client's desire to preserve basic elements of his or her diversity. Much like a caring parent, the counselor is often convinced that assimilation, to the extent that it can be achieved, will make life easier and more rewarding for the client. This may be accurate, but it is not the counselor's choice to make. I believe that the imposition of this view, if held by the counselor, would be as unethical as the imposition of any other personally held viewpoint. I prefer to regard differences in our personal worlds as issues of how, when, and with whom rather than as issues of right and wrong or appropriate and inappropriate.

Utilizing effective decision making, we are potentially able to assist our clients retain the essence of who they are as they also participate successfully in the broader community of the national culture. I believe that issues of individuation and autonomy are choices to be made by each client after careful consideration of the positive and negative consequences as in any other decision-making process we facilitate in effective counseling. However subtle or well intentioned a counselor's coercion may be, it may serve to erode trust in the counselor–client relationship, impede meaningful communication between counselor and client, and ultimately lead to an unsuccessful counseling experience.

A BASIC PARADIGM

The elements of this paradigm may seem obvious to many of you. However, without acknowledging the significance of each element, we are unlikely to achieve our goal in counseling of working in a meaningful way with each of our clients.

We must recognize and accept that there are many elements of diversity and own that it is unlikely that we know all that we *should*, or at least that we *could* know about the implications of those differences. Therefore, it is certainly prudent that we become increasingly aware of diverse values, behaviors, and goals. However, awareness as an end in itself can become an albatross around a counselor's neck, possibly providing both counselor and client with little more than discomfort.

So awareness needs to move to the next step, the acquisition of information about issues and elements of diversity. However, even being knowledgeable is only a step in a productive direction. Knowledge, without the skill to apply that knowledge, may be intellectually satisfying, but it is of limited value in the counseling process. Competence of application must be the objective that we strive toward as we mature in our ability to counsel more and more effectively.

The paradigm that I propose is obvious and simple to describe but it is a model that requires great commitment. It requires time, effort, and practice if we are to achieve a high level of competence in addressing the diversity of our clients.

Awareness → Knowledge → Competence

■ Awareness of all manner of differences that may exist within the population of clients we serve.

■ Utilization of those awarenesses to propel us to become informed of the nuances of language, behaviors, and circumstances that may affect different individuals differently.

■ Development of competence in the application of what we learn to our counseling relationships.

EVALUATING SUCCESS

There have been three factors that I have noted for myself as I have attempted to evaluate any success that I may have experienced in counseling with clients with life factors and experiences significantly different from my own.

1. The client's perception of having met his or her needs as a result of our relationship.

2. A more concrete measurement is the succession of referrals that are made to me of friends, associates, and family members of former clients with whom I have worked. I consider that to be the highest tribute of all.

3. My own sense of pleasure derived from the fascination and excitement that I experience as I see one-to-one the exquisiteness and potential harmony of the mélange rather than the indistinguishable pieces in the "melting pot."

SUMMARY ACTIVITY

1. What are the elements of diversity that you recognize in the community in which you work?

2. What would you want a counselor that you choose for yourself to know about the essence of you?

3. What might prevent you from choosing a counselor for yourself who is considerably younger or older than you?

4. What "problems" would you not bring to a counselor of the same gender as yourself? The opposite gender?

5. What "biases" do you hold that you consider justifiable because they are based on "facts" that you know?

6. What considerations would you deal with in selecting a counselor for yourself who is of another race? A different religion?

7. What "cultural" conflicts have you experienced?

8. What is your view of the "melting pot" as opposed to the mélange?

CHAPTER 11

■ ■ ■ ■ ■ ▬▬▬▬▬▬▬▬▬▬▬▬▬▬▬▬▬▬▬

INTEGRATING
METHODOLOGY WITH
THE ART OF COUNSELING

When I was a child, every household in my neighborhood that could possibly afford to have a piano had one. Many were used to fill a blank living room wall or to feature a silk-embroidered shawl covered with family photographs. Some were so beat up and worn by the passage of time and use by novice musicians that they were merely tolerated for their utilitarian purposes. Whether they were magnificent pieces of furniture or eyesores, they were basically there to lure the future pianists that the children of the family were to become.

My family's apartment was no exception. The old upright graced the living room, accompanied by the piano stool with the seat that was fun to spin up and down when no one else was around. There was no family discussion about whether or not I was to have piano lessons. Piano lessons were a nonnegotiable fact of life.

Mrs. Brandenburg arrived at the same time on the same day of every week to train me in the "art" of playing the piano, and I was to practice, practice, practice. I did exactly what I was taught. I learned the notes. I understood the signs. I played the tunes. However, as much as I learned and as well as I did, Mrs. Brandenburg rarely smiled.

After several years of this ritual, Mrs. Brandenburg announced with blatant honesty that she saw no purpose in continuing my lessons, and she recommended to my family that they relinquish their dreams of my performing at Carnegie Hall. Her parting statement was one I will never forget. In essence, she said that I was an accomplished technician. I hit the right keys, and my head and my hands worked well together, but my music had no heart. She was right. I was doing what the book said to do, but my heart didn't come through in the doing. It was not art although it was technically correct. I never became a pianist.

The point of my story is that practice does not necessarily make one anything other than practiced. "There's gotta be heart." Similarly, I believe that most people can learn counseling techniques, but only some people will become effective counselors. The most fundamental requisite for effective counseling is heart. Heart is the respect and caring for the people with whom we work. Heart is knowing that we cannot feel another person's pain but that, in our humanity, we can feel for their pain and join them on their journey through it. Heart is sharing our learned techniques so that they can be learned and employed by others. Heart is saying "good-bye" so that our clients can proceed alone having benefited from our sharing. Heart is what drew us to the counseling profession long before we learned about counseling theories and counseling techniques.

THE BASIC INGREDIENT

The most effective counseling happens when we take from our counseling texts and our counseling classes and round out the edges with our caring and our humanity. The textbooks we read, the classes and workshops we attend, give us the understandings that we need and the techniques that we can employ, but they cannot give us the heart we need to make it work. It's the communication of heart that turns technique into art.

Every field of endeavor has its artists, even when the job title includes the word *technician*. The lab technician who thinks about the impact on the person receiving the test results will work differently than the technician who only sees a specimen. The teacher who loves to see kids grow, not the person who becomes a teacher to have summers for vacation, will bring caring and love to the job. The parents who love being with their children, not the parents who stay home primarily to supervise their children, are likely to be more effective parents. The people who stand back momentarily to admire and appreciate the results of their efforts are likely to have brought the artist in themselves to the task.

NATURE VERSUS NURTURE

So, was Mrs. Brandenburg really right? Could I possibly have learned to play the piano with heart? Was it a given that I was capable of only hitting the right keys? If she had helped me look for and find the feelings that I experience when I listen to well-performed music, we might have found the key to a more artistic performance, not necessarily great talent, but a more heartfelt performance.

I think that we can find the art of counseling in ourselves if we take the time to look for it, to attend to it, and to nurture it. Most of us were drawn to the counseling profession by the encouragement of others who saw us as helpful, caring, and compassionate people. They viewed us as good listeners.

What motivated us to be these things if not heart? What sometimes happens to those exemplary qualities when we focus on and get bogged down in the jargon and techniques of our training? I believe that they can get temporarily overshadowed by the new knowledge in our head, much as the deliberate task of decoding notes will limit a smooth performance.

In this text, I've asked you to examine how you begin a counseling session. What do you say? What don't you say? I've asked you to consider the use of silence, the purpose of interruptions, the questions you ask, and the questions you avoid. I've asked you to regard the teaching of decision-making skills and communication skills as important elements in what counseling is about. I've asked that you consider the power of words and the way in which you terminate your counseling relationships. Now I'm asking you to bring back your "heart" and attach the humanity that brought you to our profession in the first place to each and every "technique" of your choice. We need only to stand still long enough and reach deep enough inside ourselves to find the feelings and then bring our heads and our hearts together. Doing this will soften the edges of learned techniques, clarify for us which theoretical constructs fit who we are, determine which population of clients we are best suited to counsel, and help us integrate the methodology of counseling into an art form.

For example, consider some of the jargon used in our profession. What do you mean when you say, establish *rapport,* establish *trust,* demonstrate *empathy, facilitate* the process? This is textbook talk. How can we achieve the goals expressed by these words more artfully? How can we add heart to the techniques to achieve artistry as counselors? Remember what you value. Remember what motivated you to enter the counseling profession.

STYLE

There is yet another issue to consider when we think of art. It is the issue of style. I consider "style" to be acquired behaviors rather than behavioral characteristics with which we were born. If this is so, it would then follow that we develop our counseling style as we mature in our profession. I remember the struggle in my early years as a counselor trying to find the style that would work for me. My experience went something like this:

I first worked under the tutelage of a professor who was about as laid back as any counselor I've seen since. His style was to promote self-discovery for the client regardless of the time it took or how arduous the path. What a model for me to emulate! My hero!

Then I worked under the supervision of another professor whose style was almost the antithesis of the first. His style was highly confrontive. He left no stone unturned. He was right in the thick of things at all times. What punch! What a model for me to emulate! My hero! Therein the struggle.

You may read this and think to yourself that this sounds perfectly ridiculous. Had you been there with me you might even have told me just to be myself. Let me tell you that, as a fledgling counselor, I didn't yet know who "myself" was.

As it turned out, I took bits and pieces from each of my models, and I continue to do so as I meet new models in my evolution and become a counselor exactly like no other because I'm developing "myself." My counseling style has developed into a synthesis of the values that I hold dear to my heart, the tried and true techniques that I have learned and sometimes modified, the behaviors that have been modeled for me, and some that seemed conspicuously absent though valuable in my opinion. This has become the ongoing development of my style that contributes to the advancement of my "art." My "art" is communication of me beyond the application of counseling techniques.

There is no one *right* way. There are many ways that can be equally effective. Just as in music, many performers have presented the same symphony, each with their own style and each with success. Ask yourself,

Who are your models?

What are your thoughts about the value of self-discovery and development?

How patient are you willing to be with yourself?

What's your "style" now?

How will you know when you're being "yourself"?

How do you adapt who you are to the techniques that you have been taught?

We can further complicate the issue of counseling artistry if we accept the premise that at some level and to some degree most humans are caring beings. Ergo, most counselors are likely to be caring people, particularly because they self-selected to train for the counseling profession. So, what's the issue?

COMMUNICATING CARING

Techniques plus caring should equal counseling artistry. How come it doesn't always work that way? As with my lack of artistry at playing the piano, I believe the problem relates to effectively communicating caring rather than whether or not caring exists. We teach communication skills to our clients, but do we work as diligently to integrate those skills into our own behavior as we do to learn them and teach them to others? We teach couples and families to communicate empathically with one another, but do we do it, or do we talk about it?

As counselors in the lifelong process of growing professionally, we have the unique opportunity to apply what we learn to our own personal development, which then comes full circle to enhance our professional abilities. This does not happen by chance. As with our clients, whom we encourage to create opportunities whereby they can practice, practice, practice their learning, we must also commit to practice in every possible arena. We can then, through the integration and internalization of the techniques we've learned—added to the style we cultivate and the "heart" we can communicate—develop into the effective counseling professionals we aim to become and contribute to the art of counseling.

SUMMARY ACTIVITY

Take some time alone. Sit back, relax, and think about how you arrived at the decision to train for and become a part of the counseling profession. To get started, ask yourself these questions:

1. Were you drawn to the people you knew with concerns and problems sometimes bigger than they could handle?
2. Was the pain you experienced as a result of dysfunctions in your family your motivating factor?
3. Were there people problems that you saw or experienced that you wanted to "fix"?
4. Did your heart go out to the disadvantaged, the lonely, the sick, the down-sized, the persecuted, the confused?
5. Was it your head, your heart, or both that influenced your choice of professions?
6. What are your thoughts and feelings about the work you're doing now?
7. Do you care about your clients? What do you mean? How do you demonstrate your caring so they can *feel* cared about?
8. What can you do that you're not already doing to bring more heart into your counseling so that what you do personifies the "artist" in you?

CHAPTER 12

TAKING CARE OF YOURSELF

Most counselors bring a combination of attributes to our profession deserving of acclamation. They care about the well-being of their clients, and they display a level of integrity that is manifested in their work as they maintain confidentiality, make appropriate referrals, and terminate the client–counselor relationship in a timely and constructive manner. Additionally, they teach life skills whereby they demonstrate their belief in the possibility of change through awareness, education, and personal power. They work diligently, driven by the contention that the emotional quality of lives can be improved, perhaps, even, that the total quality of someone's life can be improved.

If we were collectively to accept what I've written about the attributes of counselors, how do we then account for the number of counselors who burn out, experience high levels of stress, stop growing professionally, and experience chaos in their own lives? The answer that I've found for myself is in the words of the religious philosopher Hillel, who said, "if I am not for myself, who is for me; and being for my own self what am I? If not now when?"

His words are not, by any means, meant to imply a lack of caring for others. On the contrary, they remind us that we also matter and that our caring and our motivation to help must not be at the cost of excluding ourselves. With this in mind, I've selected several aspects of "taking care of yourself" that I consider important to our overall well-being and longevity as effective counselors.

PROFESSIONAL GROWTH

Growing in a vacuum is a difficult thing to do. Based on my limited knowledge of biological science, it may even be impossible. To choose to not grow is to remain stagnant while the world around us moves on and leaves us behind and out of step. If we choose to grow professionally we are confronted by the important issue of how we can continue to further develop our counseling skills once our academic/training programs are completed. I am certain that time alone will not do it. We tend to practice what we know, and what we know at any given time may not be as effective as what we can still learn. Once again, I am referring to a process, the process of staying alive and well in our chosen profession.

There are very few people I know who continue to read textbooks beyond their formal education. Those who do are usually academicians who are seeking to update their classroom text or update a bibliography of resources for their students. Rarely do these individuals read these texts as thoroughly as they expect them to be read by their students. The reason is, quite simply, that it is unlikely that there will be much that is contained in these books that will be new information. It is more likely that the information that has been well established in the counseling field might be given some new vocabulary and a different bias, but rarely is there a new discovery presented that will revolutionize the counseling profession. So, what should professional counselors read and do that will excite their thinking and enhance their professional growth? There are several things you can do. First, scan rather than peruse the professional journals. I recommend scanning for inspiration. Find a new way of addressing an issue that a colleague has put forth. Bypass the articles that represent old music with new words. Such articles may bore you as much as they bore me, and, too often, they represent the author's need to publish rather than the desire to excite colleagues with a new perspective or methodology. Second, read newspapers like the Science section of the *New York Times*. Often, you'll find information relevant to our work as counselors. Most of the time, it is news! How exciting to come on new information, new theories, new concerns, and new possibilities for our work as psychological helpers. Third, scan the popular magazines so that you can remain current with the issues that are important to the general public. Sometimes the covers alone will remind you of the struggles that people address everyday, being too fat, too thin, alone, lonely, aging, experiencing career changes, loss, gender conflicts, having or not having sex and relationships, money, self-esteem, going bald, raising children, watching children leave the nest, and on, and on, and on. These are the concerns that sell magazines. These are your client's real-life issues.

Fourth, check out the best-selling books at the bookstore. What's the latest self-help book that is leaping off the shelf? What are the anxieties that novelists are addressing that are shared by the greatest number of people? Keep abreast of what your clients want to know and to which issues they relate. Think about the possible implications. Fifth, attend workshops that present topics about which you know the least. You surely will grow the most by opening your mind to information that is different from what you already know or to a perspective different from your own or a question asked that you hadn't thought to raise.

Sixth, critique rather than quickly move to criticize methods different from those you have learned to utilize. The old ways are not necessarily the best ways. In addition, the old ways can sometimes become so routine to us as practitioners that we might even become sloppy in their application. Continue to critically examine theories and practices that you have previously dismissed as unworkable for you. Know what has turned you against these techniques. I consider this openness to resemble the brainstorming that we advocate for our clients. What are the possibilities beyond the methods you have routinely employed? What is there about these other methods that might suit your style, your values, your objectives? What is it about these methods that causes you to reject them as a part of your counseling repertoire? Know what your reasons are for including or excluding specific techniques. I believe that this ongoing evaluation of how we do what we do helps to keep us current, involved, and passionate about our work.

Seventh, talk with other counselors. What are they doing? How are they doing it? What have they learned and what are they learning as they work with clients? Share your experiences with other counselors. Sometimes talking about what you're doing can help clarify your methods, even for you.

Eighth, take courses in areas of study that you missed along the way. We have all been trained in programs that have a finite number of credits required for completion of our study. Surely, we are all grateful for that. The negative side of this situation, however, is that there is always so much more that we could have studied that is also relevant to our work. How satisfied are you that you understand the mores of the people with whom you work who come from cultures that are different from your own? What do you know about the aging process and issues of death and dying? How knowledgeable are you about family issues, e.g., dispute resolution, family violence, addictions, disabilities, and so on? What do you know about the appropriate use of psychodramatic techniques, hypnosis, and neurolinguistic programming? None of us will ever know everything there is to know, but we can surely include the acquisition of knowledge into the process of our professional growth.

Finally, practice what you teach. I can't imagine what could facilitate more professional growth than your own personal growth. I believe that the more effectively I communicate, the more effectively I can teach communication skills. The more effectively I incorporate the elements of decision making in my own life, the more effectively I can impart the process to my clients. The more I strive toward congruence in my daily life by examining my thoughts, feelings, and behaviors, the greater the likelihood that I will successfully facilitate this harmony for others. The more I take care of myself, the greater and clearer my purpose becomes in helping others care for themselves.

SUPERVISION

As counseling professionals, many of us are privileged to have supervisors who can promote an ongoing learning environment. Unfortunately, not all of us are so privileged. Some of us may be straddled with supervisors who know less about effective counseling than we do, or supervisors who come from an orientation very different from our own who may not be open to differing approaches. All too often, counselors find themselves being supervised by individuals with no training in counseling skills at all. These can be people who have been trained in administration, supervision, or organizational management. With all due respect to their expertise, it has been my experience that their interests are primarily quantitative. They are likely to assess counselors and counseling sessions in terms of how many? How often? How long? The quality of counseling is not theirs to judge, as this falls outside of their training. How does qualitative supervision take place under these circumstances?

My point here is not to dispute the ability of counselors to learn beyond skills training classes. As I've said, we attend workshops, we read books and professional journals, and we talk with other counselors. The point is that we may or may not integrate into our counseling behaviors those skills that we have only been exposed to at the level of cognition. To put it another way, we may be able "to talk the talk" but can we effectively "walk the walk"?

As counselors we are no different than our clients who are also learning and practicing new skills. We need to be able to critique our performance, and we need support along the way. Generally, many of us bring some level of anxiety to each new counseling relationship. This may never leave us entirely. After all, the unknown is the unknown and each new client is, initially, unknown.

In a perfect situation, a well-trained, highly effective supervisor would be present during our counseling sessions and would assist, critique, and support us. Obviously, this would violate confidentiality and potentially demean our expertise in the eyes of the client. So, let's dispose of the "perfect" situation as unfeasible beyond training programs.

Supervision can be bought. We can select another professional counselor for whom we have high regard, and we can purchase time in the same way that clients purchase counseling time. We can share situations with our supervisor and discuss alternate routes that may be taken in our counseling sessions. We can set goals for ourselves just as our clients do, and, with the support of supervision, we can work toward these goals. The obstacles that may exist would be the extent of our willingness to commit time, energy, and money to the process.

Yet another possibility is to join with other counselors, in a group of four to six, who will meet regularly to discuss cases and concerns with one another. This can be an opportunity to share success stories as well as frustrations, to role play alternate options that had not been employed, to learn from one another, and to give and receive support. All that is required is the commitment of time and energy with no financial burden attached.

Last, but not least, is a process that I call "self-critiquing." This involves periodic audiotaping of our own counseling sessions with appropriate client consent. Further, it involves the establishment of a list of behavioral objectives that we each establish for ourselves as we listen and critique our taped counseling sessions. Most important in this process is that the behavioral objectives established are *by the counselor, for the counselor,* and not the client. This is a process of self-supervision that eliminates a cost factor that may cause some of us not to buy supervision. It can also be the least intimidating form of supervision because it is a private process. However, it absolutely requires a commitment of time and a standard of counseling that we have individually accepted as representative of effective counseling and against which we are committed to measuring our growth. The process of self-supervision that I'm setting out for your consideration is a fluid process. It requires change as you succeed in meeting previously established objectives.

THE SELF-CRITIQUING PROCESS

Let's suppose that you have received your client's permission to tape your counseling session and, in fact, have done so. Let's further suppose that you have agreed with my previously stated position that *why* questions are potentially nonproductive. Now, you listen to your taped session and you hear yourself unwittingly ask an abundance of questions that begin with *why.* How many, specifically—ten, twenty, more?

Now let's say that you don't like what you heard yourself doing. Perhaps you hadn't even realized that you were doing this. It's time for you to write a *reasonable* behavioral objective for yourself in the same way that you would encourage your client to establish behavioral goals. *Reasonable* is now the operative word. If you heard twenty uses of *why,* it is not reasonable to set your goal at zero. You are much too likely to fail to meet your goal, and failing will not be any more pleasant or encouraging for you than it would be for your client. Therefore, you want to be reasonable toward yourself. Then you need to follow the same format you would use if you were facilitating goal setting with your client.

The Necessary Components of Behavioral Objectives

You can begin to formulate your plan with a statement of ownership and commitment, "I will ," a description of what you will do, "ask *why* questions," set a standard of how you will measure your success, "a maximum of ten times," and the time you will do it, "in my next counseling session." Your resulting behavioral objective is, I will ask a maximum of ten *why* questions in my next counseling session. Because this objective pertains to your behavior, you can commit to it for your next session whether or not you are working with the same client. If you succeed in meeting this objective, you can reduce the frequency further for ensuing sessions. You are now on your way to improving your skills, and that is likely to please you.

There is no behavioral objective that I can imagine that is too simplistic. It is a valuable goal if you value the behavior in counseling and you want to minimize or maximize your use of the behavior. Other aspects of counseling behavior can be targeted in the same way.

- Establishing rapport: I will address my client by name a minimum of four times in my next counseling session.
- Effective use of language: I will say *feel* when I mean *think* a maximum of twice in my next counseling session.
- Facilitating client focus: I will interrupt my client by saying, "I don't understand how that connects to what you said a minute ago," when I hear my client going off on a tangent.
- Improving warm-up: I will engage my client in small talk during the first minute of each session by asking open-ended questions about the weather, the ride over, and so forth.

Now listen to the tape of your next session. Listen carefully in terms of the objective you established for yourself. How effective were you in meeting your goal? Perhaps it was more difficult than you expected. What would you ask your client if this were your client's objective? How will you modify your objective for next time? What else did you hear that you want to work on? What will your behavioral objectives be for the next counseling session? To what extent do these objectives also apply in your life outside of counseling? How can you restate these objectives so you can consciously bring them to interactions in your personal life for additional practice?

Remember that old, ingrained ways are not easily changed or eliminated. Be as patient with yourself as you would be with a client. The guiding principle is practice, practice, practice. In my opinion, there is no acceptable excuse that I can think of for professional stagnation. In fact, I truly believe that, if we choose not to grow, we will inadvertently lose ground. I also suspect that we will become bored with what we're doing, which will add to our ineffectiveness. Rather than allowing that to happen, we need to continually challenge ourselves to acquire greater skills, which will generate greater pride in ourselves as effective and dynamic counselors. I believe that this process of professional self-actualization will not progress without some significant and consistent supervision. Furthermore, as with any actualization process, it is never ending and often wonderfully satisfying. The number of clients seen or the dollars earned is not the measure of successful counseling. There's much more to being a counselor than that.

ETHICS

There are ethical standards superimposed in most, if not all, professions, and the counseling profession is no exception. It is unlikely that our professional codes of ethics would cause a problem for most of us except by omission, which we know very well is an unacceptable excuse. Therefore, it is implicit that we read and accept our professional codes as the ethical guides for the work that we do and the manner in which we deliver our services. The complete codes of ethics are available from the National Board for Certified Counselors (NBCC) and the American Counseling Association (ACA) (see references).

Although reading a document of this kind may not be at the top of your list of things you can hardly wait to read, I strongly recommend that you put it there. Read it. Think about each item that pertains to the counseling that you offer. Reflect on any items that may in any way conflict with your personal values. Discuss these selected items with your colleagues for their interpretations. Work through any conflicts that you may have so that you can go forward with your work confident that your procedures are ethically sound and endorsed by our profession. I consider this to be an important aspect of taking care of yourself. I consider it to be a professional, as well as a personal, responsibility.

SELF-EXPLORATION

Taking care of myself requires that I understand where I am and who I am at a specific time in my life. What I need, what I want, and where I want to be are objectives that can only meaningfully be established from a basic understanding of myself rooted in the present.

I see two different levels that require my attention if I am to take care of myself. The first of these necessitates that I examine my day-to-day process. The second is that I establish goals for myself for the next year or longer, depending on where I am in my career and in my life.

The daily schedule that circumscribes a counselor's routine is generally prescribed by the clock, and almost always fluctuates somewhere between difficult and more difficult. The counseling profession requires that you be dedicated to your work, skillful at what you do, caring, accepting, congruent, involved, and so on. This is hardly the description of an easy day's work. It is the kind of work that has the potential to take all that you have to give and give very little immediate gratification in return. So, how do you feed the elements of your own being so that you can return to it day after day successfully? Let's look at the day-to-day process in terms of mind, body, and spirit.

Mind

How do I leave "work" at work? I asked my students who are presently working as counselors and their responses included, "Distance myself" and "Wash everything out of my head." These are important goals, but how do you achieve them? Consider the following possibilities and then add your own ideas.

- Stay at work as long as needed to complete reports and other paperwork and then do *not* take work home.
- Take time in your car, on the bus, or train to focus on where you're going and what you'll do when you get there rather than where you've been all day and what you've been doing.
- Take the long way home on your most stressed days to afford yourself the additional separating time that you may need and deserve.
- Change your clothes when you get home and get out of your counseling uniform. Put on play clothes, fun clothes, family clothes, or loafing clothes.
- Call a friend or speak with a family member about their day, *not* yours.
- Listen to music that you associate with fun.
- Initiate a "pity party" with no invited guests. All that's required is that you complain out loud about all the injustices of the world (including how you were treated at the office today). Complain about everything you give and how little you get. The most important elements of this "party" are that you set an alarm clock (or oven timer) for twenty minutes before you begin and, when time is up, the party ends and you then go do something you enjoy. Feeling sorry for yourself and feeling angry are natural experiences for all of us. The only question is, Are these feelings in charge or are you in charge? You call the shots when you throw the party.
- Last, but not least, remind yourself that life is more than a series of meetings and counseling sessions. Look around you and find testimony to what I've said. You might be taking your work and yourself too seriously.

Body

What parts of your body worked especially hard today? Did you stand on your feet all day or perhaps you tired your back sitting at the computer? Did you work alone all day and now you want to feel the warmth of touch from another being?

- Exercise the muscles you didn't use all day. Take a walk, shoot baskets, ride a bike, work out, stretch and breathe, dance, clean the house, move, move, move!
- Give your body a treat (whatever that is for you): a warm relaxing bath, a hot shower, a cold shower, a cup of coffee, tea, or cocoa.
- Hug your children.
- Hug your partner.
- Hug your pet.

- Brush your hair.
- Take a nap (twenty minutes can do the trick).
- Wash your car.
- Get a neck and shoulder massage (more if you can).

Spirit

Do anything that delights or challenges you that is totally and unquestionably unrelated to counseling. Add your own to the following suggestions:

- Cook.
- Work in your shop building something.
- Do a puzzle.
- Find something to laugh about.
- Do the laundry.
- Pair your socks or stockings, and discard the ones that have holes or rips.
- Take a course in mythology, a foreign language, pottery, golf, whatever.
- Water your plants.
- Rake leaves.
- Sing a song.
- Remember, also, to plan periodic vacations. A weekend away can be as healthy as three weeks if you make it so. Enjoy the planning and the anticipation that you can milk from it by letting yourself savor the thought of time away. Just one admonition before you plan: By definition *vacation*, a time of rest and recreation away from one's work or school; a holiday, attendance at workshops or conventions does not qualify as vacation time.

I believe that, if we do not deliberately refuel ourselves, we will run out of steam. Counseling is a depleting profession. We give of ourselves to others with no expectation that they will return the favor. My concern is that, if we do not systematically remove ourselves from our day's work and focus on caring for ourselves, we will be so starved for nurturance that we might bring excessive and inappropriate demands to our personal relationships. This is neither a healthy nor happy prospect.

Let's look now at the less immediate caretaking and consider what you want for yourself in the near future. Here's a wonderful opportunity for you to apply to yourself the very process you teach to your clients. The technique that works best for me is to paint a picture, first in my mind's eye and then with words on paper. I begin by asking myself questions that require specific answers.

- What do I want to be doing professionally that I'm not doing now?
- What will doing that give me that I don't presently receive?

- What does it require for me to get there?
- How much control do I have over the requirements?
- What do I need to do to make this picture a reality?
- What will the cost of this process be physically, emotionally, and financially?
- What will the cost be if I choose not to put this process into action?
- How do I begin?
- When will I begin?
- How will I measure the results of my plan?

The fundamental emphasis of this self-exploration is to know who you are and who you want to become.

I am very much a creature of habit. I find security in routine and safety in what I consider to be reasonable predictability. However, within the parameters of routine and predictability, I have learned that I need and want to periodically change the routines to avoid boredom and lethargy, which can make life one big flatlined hum. I am far from all I can be without challenge and without passion. Therefore, I have chosen to design and work toward twists and curves in my professional picture rather than switching highways. I make considered modifications rather than big changes. What about you?

MEASURING SUCCESS

Let's define *success* before we consider how we can measure it and how it applies to ourselves:

> "a favorable outcome; doing what was desired or attempted; the attainment of wealth or fame or position" (OAD).

My immediate recommendation is that we begin by ignoring reference to wealth, fame, and position. These are terms not generally applied to counseling professionals. In fact, these are not generally the ambitions and goals that motivate most individuals to affiliate with our profession. What I hear most often from counselors is that they hope to derive great satisfaction from helping others. This is not at the expense of making a reasonable salary, decent working conditions, and so on. If we agree that "helping" is what we attempt to do, then we might agree that we can measure our success by the extent to which we help others, even as we help ourselves.

My position here is relatively simple. I believe that, if I can succeed in helping others learn how to more effectively help themselves to the point where they no longer need for me to facilitate the process, I have succeeded. Furthermore, I believe that if I have learned how to nurture myself and how to continue to grow, I have succeeded.

■ When a client ends the counseling relationship ready to proceed alone, and when I look forward to the next day as a new adventure with a new client, I have the measurement of success that I want.

■ When I consider a situation in a new way, or learn something I didn't know before, I have a measurement of success that I want.

■ When new clients contact me as the result of a referral by their friend or a family member, I have the external validation of success that feels terrific.

■ When I receive a Christmas card or note from a former client with a family picture of smiles, success is defined by the picture, and I know I've chosen the right profession for myself.

The measurement of success is a very personal matter. You must first decide what it is you are striving for in your career as a counselor. What are the rewards that you want for yourself? What are you striving to provide for your clients? I truly don't want to hear clients say, "I couldn't have gotten here without you." I'd much rather hear "I've got what I need and I can take care of myself now."

Success in our profession is somewhat like showing birds how to fly: You model it, you sometimes push the learning along, but you can't do it for them. Once they have learned they fly away, and that's what we are in business to achieve, isn't it?

SUMMARY ACTIVITY

1. Keep a log of your activities for a month. At the end of the month, review your log, giving particular attention to *what you did for you.*
   a. What did you do during this month to facilitate a small step forward in your professional development?
   b. How did you end each work day so that you could emerge from your counseling role?
   c. What did you do each day to nurture yourself?
   d. What have you done this month that particularly pleased you? Did you think to give yourself a pat on the back?

2. Think through your views regarding the purpose and the value of ongoing supervision.
   a. What will you strive to achieve from supervision?
   b. What do you expect from a supervisor?
   c. What will you do if supervision is not meeting your expectations?
   d. How much time, energy, and money are you willing to invest for supervision of your work?

EPILOGUE

I hope that this has been a worthwhile journey for you. I hope that you have found within the covers of the book ideas that perhaps you haven't considered; statements with which you agree; and some statements with which you take exception. If this is the case, then I am satisfied with what I've done.

If you come away from this text in any way inspired to work harder, to work more thoughtfully, and to continue to grow professionally and personally, then I am very satisfied with what I've done.

If you find some new enthusiasm and zest for our profession from what we've shared, then I am extremely satisfied with what I've done.

If we all can assist in helping others find less chaos, fewer regrets, and greater joy in their lives, then we will have made some small, but significant contribution, to our world.

If you find that joy and satisfaction permeate your counseling career, then you and I will share the satisfaction of having chosen wisely in our professional lives.

Carpe Diem!

EFFECTIVE COUNSELING
FROM A TO Z

Address client by name

Be clear, concise, and audible

Call for client's ownership of statements

Differentiate between thoughts and feelings

Eliminate *why* from your vocabulary

Facilitate the learning process

Get the main point by asking the client what it is

Honor all rules of professional ethics

Interrupt to promote focusing

Judge effectiveness rather than good versus bad or right versus wrong

Keep the focus on the client, not on people outside the session

Listen for patterns of behavior

Model using *what* and *how* questions

Note cultural influences and honor their importance

Own *your* feelings and thoughts

Pose questions that challenge the payoff of existing behaviors

Question—question—question

Refrain from storytelling

Share your confusion when hearing contradictory statements

Test your client's readiness to act by confronting inertia

Use silence to encourage client work

Vary your voice pitch to express your animation

Write notes that describe behaviors rather than experiences

Xerox this list and post it for your regular review

Yield counseling time to your client's learning, not your advice

Zero in on *your* behaviors during each counseling session

REFERENCES AND RESOURCES

REFERENCES

Axelson, John A. (1999). *Counseling and development in a multicultural society* (3rd ed.). Pacific Grove, California: Brooks/Cole.

Berenson, B. (1968). Level of therapist functioning, patient depth of self-exploration, and type of confrontations. *Journal of Counseling Psychology, 15,* 317–321.

Brammer, L. M., & MacDonald, G. (1999). *The helping relationship—process and skills* (7th ed.). Boston: Allyn and Bacon.

Carkhuff, R. R., & Berenson, B. G. (1977). *Beyond counseling and therapy* (2nd ed.). New York: Holt, Rinehart and Winston.

Cohen, E. D., & Spieler, G. (1999). *The virtuous therapist: Ethical practice of counseling and psychotherapy.* Belmont, California: Wadsworth.

Cormier, W. H., & Cormier, L. S. (1991). *Interviewing strategies for helpers* (3rd ed.). Pacific Grove, California: Brooks/Cole.

Egan, G. (1994). *The skilled helper* (5th ed.). Pacific Grove, California: Brooks/Cole.

Ellis, A., & Harper, R. A. (1975). *A new guide to rational living.* New Jersey: Prentice-Hall.

Gelso, B., & Carter, J. (1985). The relationship in counseling psychotherapy: Components, consequences, and theoretical antecedents. *The Counseling Psychologist, 13,* 155–243.

Gopaul-McNicol, S., & Thomas-Presswood, T. (1998). *Working with linguistically and culturally different children.* Boston: Allyn and Bacon.

Hansen, J. C., Rossberg, R. H., & Cramer, S. H. (1994). *Counseling: Theory and process* (5th ed.). Boston: Allyn and Bacon.

Hutchins, D. E., & Vaught, C. C. (1997). *Helping relationships and strategies* (3rd ed.). Pacific Grove, California: Brooks/Cole.

LaClave, L., & Brack, G. (1987). Reframing to deal with patient resistance: Practical applications. *American Journal of Psychotherapy, 43,* 68–76.

Littrell, J. H. (1998). *Brief counseling in action.* New York: W. W. Norton.

Martin, D. G. (1983). *Counseling and therapy skills.* Prospect Heights, Illinois: Waveland.

Maslow, A. H. (1970). *Motivation and personality* (2nd ed.). New York: Harper & Row.

Maultsby, M. C. (1984). *Rational behavior therapy.* Englewood Cliffs, New Jersey: Prentice-Hall.

May, R. (1967). *The art of counseling.* New York: Abington.

Nunnally, E. W., Miller, S., & Wackman, D. B. (1977). *Couple communication instructor manual.* Minneapolis, Minnesota: Interpersonal Communication Programs.

Oxford American Dictionary. (1980). New York: Avon.

Perls, F. (1973). *The gestalt approach and eye witness to therapy.* Palo Alto, California: Science & Behavior.

Perls, F., Hefferline, R. E., & Goodman, R. (1951). *Gestalt therapy: Excitement and growth in the human personality.* New York: Dell.

Robitschek. C. G., & McCarthy, P. R. (1991). Prevalence of counselor self reference in the therapeutic dyad. *Journal of Counseling Psychotherapy, 69,* 218–221.

Rocco Cottone, R., & Tarvydas, V. M. (1998). *Ethical and professional issues in counseling.* Upper Saddle River, New Jersey: Prentice-Hall.

Rogers, C. (1957). The necessary and sufficient conditions of therapeutic personality change. *Journal of Counseling Psychology, 21,* 95–103.

Rogers, C. (1980). *A way of being.* Boston: Houghton Mifflin.

Skovholt, Thomas M., & Ronnestad, Michael H. (1995). *The evolving professional self.* New York: John Wiley & Sons.

Young, M. E. (1998). *Learning the art of helping.* Upper Saddle River, New Jersey: Prentice-Hall.

RESOURCES

American Counseling Association, 5999 Stevenson Ave., Alexandria, VA 22304
Internet address: www.counseling.org
Phone number: 1-800-347-6647

National Board for Certified Counselors, Inc.
3-D Terrace Way
Greensboro, NC 27403